"I am so grateful for the life and witness of John Perkins. . . . Thankfully, Shane has done an excellent job taking us to the front porch to sit and receive invaluable stories and wisdom from a wise, Jesus-shaped elder of the church. *Go and Do* is gripping and inspiring, and every page invites us deeper into a life of faithful justice, healing, and transformation, which is exactly what we need right now."

—DREW G. I. HART, author of *Who Will Be a Witness?*

"Being a peacemaker is hard work. Especially in the midst of the culture wars. Is there an intersection between nonviolence and our polarized, othering, and fragmented society? Yes! John Perkins and Shane Blackshear are paving a critical path forward for us—how do we enact the way of Jesus in a world marked by the way of the beast? By God's grace, this book will impact you the way it did me."

—A. J. SWOBODA, author of *After Doubt*

"We have much to learn about peacemaking from the life and ministry of John M. Perkins. In our relationally broken world, Perkins models how to bridge the divide and love the people we least like, even hate the way Jesus did. *Go and Do* will no doubt guide Christian leaders practically to promote the peace of Jesus in their local communities."

—MICHELLE AMI REYES, author of *Becoming All Things: How Small Changes Lead to Lasting Connections across Cultures*

"With a robust understanding of the complexities of peacemaking, Shane Blackshear and John Perkins pastorally point us to the alternative way of Jesus by drawing on the richness of Scripture. Shane and John understand that peacemaking is messy and difficult, but readers' hearts and minds will be nourished and infused with God's creative and healing imagination for the world. We need this book more than ever."

—TARA BETH LEACH, author of *Radiant Church*

Go and Do

Go and Do

Nine Axioms on
Peacemaking and Transformation
from the Life of John Perkins

JOHN PERKINS &
SHANE BLACKSHEAR

 CASCADE *Books* · Eugene, Oregon

GO AND DO
Nine Axioms on Peacemaking and Transformation from the Life of John
Perkins

Cascade Books
An Imprint of Wipf and Stock Publishers
199 W. 8th Ave., Suite 3
Eugene, OR 97401

www.wipfandstock.com

PAPERBACK ISBN: 978-1-7252-9936-8
HARDCOVER ISBN: 978-1-7252-9937-5
EBOOK ISBN: 978-1-7252-9938-2

Cataloguing-in-Publication data:

Names: Perkins, John, author. Blackshear, Shane, author.

Title: Go and do : nine axioms on peacemaking and transformation from
the life of John Perkins. / John Perkins and Shane Blackshear.

Description: Eugene, OR: Cascade Books, 2022 | Includes bibliographical
references.

Identifiers: ISBN 978-1-7252-9936-8 (paperback) | ISBN 978-1-7252-9937-5
(hardcover) | ISBN 978-1-7252-9938-2 (ebook)

Subjects: LCSH: Perkins, John M., 1930–. | Race relations—Religious
aspects—Christianity. | African Americans—Civil rights—History—
20th century.

Classification: E185.615 .G60 2022 (print) | E185 (ebook)

Contents

Abbreviations

KJV   King James Version

MLF   Mobile Loaves and Fishes

Introduction

Go and Do Likewise

ONE OF THE MOST famous passages in the Bible is found in Luke 10:25–37. Jesus tells the story of the Good Samaritan. If, like me (Shane), you grew up in church, you know the story well. It's long been a favorite in children's church gatherings in part because it's a simple and easy to understand story, with a simple and easy to understand lesson: be kind and take care of others. While being kind and taking care of others is certainly important and consistent with Christian teaching, there's much more to this story and a far more radical narrative is at hand.

Let's start with the actual text.

> Just then a lawyer stood up to test Jesus. "Teacher," he said, "what must I do to inherit eternal life?" He said to him, "What is written in the law? What do you read there?" He answered, "You shall love the Lord your God with all your heart, and with all your soul, and with all your strength, and with all your mind; and your neighbor as yourself." And he said to him, "You have given the right answer; do this, and you will live."
>
> But wanting to justify himself, he asked Jesus, "And who is my neighbor?" Jesus replied, "A man was going down from Jerusalem to Jericho, and fell into the hands of robbers, who stripped him, beat him, and went away, leaving him half dead. Now by chance a priest was going down that road; and when he saw him, he passed by on

the other side. So likewise a Levite, when he came to the place and saw him, passed by on the other side. But a Samaritan while traveling came near him; and when he saw him, he was moved with pity. He went to him and bandaged his wounds, having poured oil and wine on them. Then he put him on his own animal, brought him to an inn, and took care of him. The next day he took out two denarii, gave them to the innkeeper, and said, 'Take care of him; and when I come back, I will repay you whatever more you spend.' Which of these three, do you think, was a neighbor to the man who fell into the hands of the robbers?" He said, "The one who showed him mercy." Jesus said to him, "Go and do likewise."[1]

That's the story and you've probably heard it read aloud several times, but it's worth the trouble to pause here and ask some questions of the text. The Good Samaritan was not the man's name, it's a description.

So, who were the Samaritans? To answer this we have to go way back hundreds of years before Jesus when the Hebrews, God's chosen people, had their northern kingdom of Israel captured by the Assyrians. This was a devastating blow to the Israelites. Some of them were taken into captivity and some were left behind. Some of those that were left behind intermarried with the Assyrians. This was forbidden by God, not to mention the perceived act of betrayal it was to enter into marriage with those that conquered your own land and people. These unfaithful and treasonous Hebrews and their children were Samaritans.

The Samaritans were marked people—marked for their failure to be good and faithful. Jews and Samaritans, as a rule, didn't even talk to each other. This is why in the story of Jesus and the Samaritan woman at the well,[2] when Jesus asks the woman to give him a drink of water, it's not a small thing. Jesus not only spoke to a Samaritan (not to mention a woman, which would have also broken social taboos), but actually puts himself in a place of needing something from her. The audacity of Jesus' request is exposed

1. Luke 10:25–37.
2. John 4:1–42.

when she responds, "How is it that you, a Jew, ask a drink of me, a woman of Samaria?"[3]

The next question we should ask about the story of the Good Samaritan is: Who was Jesus talking to? The answer is given in verse 25, "a lawyer," or as the New International Version puts it "an expert in the law,"[4] in this case Jewish law. The expert would have been surrounded by other experts or at least other Jewish people. This is important because Jesus would have been talking to the very people that would have seen Samaritans as their enemy.

It may be difficult to put yourself in the shoes of Jesus' original audience, but to make it easier, reread the parable but insert the name of a group that you see as an enemy or at least find it difficult to love. The group will be different for different people, but will probably stand for a cause you find abhorrent: gun control, gun rights, pro-life, pro-choice, environmentalists, lobbyists, Democrats, Republicans, the Taliban, Isis, or people who wear cargo shorts. Take your pick. Now, reread the story, making your worst enemy the hero. It reads differently, doesn't it? Now, you have an idea of how this story landed for those in Jesus' audience that day.

Another important component of the story is that Jesus didn't initially tell it at all. Jesus seems to have been happy just to tell his audience to "love the Lord your God with all your heart, and with all your soul, and with all your mind."[5] Often our response is like the response of the lawyer, "You're telling me to love my neighbor? Okay then, who exactly is my neighbor?" And what we're really asking is "Who exactly am I required to love and who can I get by with not loving?" The story of the Good Samaritan is an answer to a question in the classic style of a Jewish rabbi, not content to just give a straight answer but to instead tell a story that allows the hearer to engage and come to the answer on a deeper level. By the end of it, Jesus is directing the question to the lawyer, and this Jewish lawyer has to admit that the Samaritan, his enemy, was the real neighbor.

3. John 4:9.

4. Luke 10:25.

5. Luke 10:27b.

In effect, the answer to the lawyer's question "And who is my neighbor?"[6] is "Your enemy, the person you like the least, the person you hate, and everyone!"

The story of the Good Samaritan is instructive to us in many ways, not least of which in the way that the Samaritan was not passive. We tend to think of peacemaking as a passive endeavor. Not rocking the boat, not causing waves. We shrink back, we withhold ourselves for the sake of "peace." These actions are of course not real peacemaking, they're a false peace and a false unity. Real peacemaking is risky, dangerous, and costly.

The Life of John Perkins

John and I (Shane) spent some two years sitting down with each other, from our respective homes in different parts of the country, having conversations about John's life. After those two years (plus a few additional later conversations) we identified nine key aspects of his story that we felt were crucial and instrumental in building a life and lifestyle of peacemaking and transformation, both deeply important and often overlooked components of loving God with all our heart, soul, strength, mind, and loving our neighbor as ourself. It's our hope that John's life can be your guide as you figure out what living this Jesus-life means to you in your context.

6. Luke 10:29b.

CHAPTER 1

Know Where
and Who You Came From

A Son of Sharecroppers

I (SHANE) SAT IN the counselor's office thinking about how I ended up there. I was in my early twenties, had recently become a pastor of a church I was planting with a few friends, and I was desperate to change some patterns in my life. My biggest problem was that I was angry, almost all of the time. If someone cut me off in traffic I fumed. My rage wasn't just reserved for strangers, those on my church planting team were targets too. If a team member didn't show up for an event or workday I secretly judged and resented them. Blowing up and yelling at them seemed unbecoming of a pastor, so instead I seethed internally, becoming quiet and withdrawn. The result was downward spirals of isolation, resentment, and bitterness.

I had done what I was told was required of me to become a Christian earlier in my life, namely, praying a prayer to accept Jesus as my personal Lord and Savior. I had walked down the aisle of my church and gotten baptized when I was six years old. When I was twelve I began having massive doubts about God's existence, and even if there *was* a God I wasn't sure about my standing with him. The good news is that at the end of some gut-wrenching wrestling with doubt I ultimately came out on the other side with a more real and serious faith in a more relational God. And yet, even then, that experience alone hadn't prepared me for much of the nitty-gritty of life, specifically the struggles I seemed to experience with anger. It seemed that an experience with God, and my sincerity, weren't enough on their own.

As I sat in that counselor's waiting room that day, I would have told you that my rage came from a place of justice. I was simply angry at people not behaving as they should, not following through with their commitments, being selfish, and putting their desires before others.

That day the counselor patiently helped me unpack what had been going on inside of me. The acuteness and constancy of my anger eventually subsided. Years passed, and I was better and happier, and while my anger was there it wasn't perennial. I still struggled with understanding why and how it had held such a tight grip on me. This was just one of the things weighing on me when I met John Perkins.

John Shares: Where He Came From

The first day I met John he was in Austin to speak at a conference. We met up in his hotel room downtown. I sat on the sofa in his room and he in a puffy chair to the side. I had just met John for the first time in person a few minutes earlier, as he ate breakfast downstairs in the lobby. I knew a lot about John but only from reading his books. I had only heard his voice in the YouTube videos I watched of his sermons and talks. Suffice it to say that I was a little nervous meeting him in person. Truthfully, I really wanted him to like me.

Lucky for me, John seems to like almost everyone he meets. Seconds after meeting someone new he'll start talking about the last conference he went to, a sermon he's working on, or the latest news about his wife or grandchildren, as if you've been friends for years and he's just catching up on the latest goings-on of his life.

There we were in that typical midrange big city hotel room sitting on a couch and chair that no doubt looked just like the couch and chair in every room in the building. I was still nervous to be sitting across from someone I so admired and so larger than life. I tried to act casual.

"So, Dr. Perkins," I tried to say as nonchalantly as possible, "what was your childhood like?"

He stared off nowhere in particular as if trying to think of where to start.

"Well, you know, it seems like now, as I reflect back, my grandmother had been the mother of nineteen children, my grandfather was already dead when I was born in 1930. We had been sharecroppers and bootleggers. Of the nineteen children, many of the girls had babies and they said they had been married to some man, but they weren't around. So, when my mother died, my daddy dropped me off at my grandmother's house along with these other children. So it was a big house. I guess the first thing I remember, probably, was crying, looking for a person to care. I'm sure my grandmother loved me. I would always cry in her lap. I was probably crying saying 'Momma,' because the first thing I remember knowing was that my mother was dead. I didn't have a mother to call upon. I think there was a heavy feeling of sorrow around me." His voice was taking on the cadence of a sermon the more he talked about his mother.

"As I look back at having lived this life, that deficit of cradle love from my mother probably set the course of my life. Now that I think about it, I think it was that longing for love and acceptance, deep belonging, I didn't understand it at the time, where I was going, but I was being shaped by that and the desire to be loved."

I was taken aback by John's awareness of how his very early experiences in his family of origin had profound effects on the rest of his life.

John has shared the story of his mother's death publicly in the past. She had a disease called pellagra, and it was caused by a lack of the vitamin niacin in the diet or the body's inability to absorb niacin. During that time, it was an epidemic in the United States and caused over 100,000 deaths.

What took me aback was that I could see that for John, it was still fresh, and it shaped his outlook on life from a young age. He told me about how his mother's sickness had played a role in the way he saw his place in the world.

As he often does when recalling something, John squinted his eyes shut and looked down and to the side as he talked. "Probably less than ten years ago I was having my early morning prayer and Bible study with my youngest daughter. She was taking over my ministry and I was trying to anchor her in the story of the Bible. I had been studying and discipling people in the Bible for forty years probably, and that morning we were studying the Gospel of John. In the text, John 19:26–27, Jesus was on the cross and said 'this is your son'[1] to his mother and said to John 'this is your mother.'[2] There was this exchange, and it hit me then. My mother died. This is a similar thing. Jesus is about to die. It's a similar exchange. Jesus takes care of his mother before he dies. My mother died, and I was taken care of and I said 'I was probably taking the nutrition she needed for her life.' She needed protein, and I was nursing, taking it from her. I stood up, looking at my daughter and I said something like 'I killed my mother!' You know, very emotional like." His head bobbed as he talked as if to emphasize the impact his realization had on him that day.

"My daughter put her arms around me and she said, 'It happened exactly the way she would have wanted it to happen.' It's true, my mother would have *chosen* to give her life so I would live. In that realization that morning, I saw myself as being an absolutely successful person." His voice rose with those last three words. He knew he had lived up to the hope his mother had for him.

John so clearly saw the connection between his later decisions and the story of his mother. "That was always fuel for my success too, that thought, one day she would ask me, 'What did you do for people like me?' So that responsibility, that debt to my mother, all

1. John 19:26.
2. John 19:27.

came together, and it has sort of shaped my life. It was an emotional moment in my life, cause—um—I don't know, I couldn't fault my mother for dying on me, I had to take responsibility, I couldn't fault my grandmother for taking care of all those grandchildren. I remember seeing my father mark an X for his name and I realized he couldn't read or write, so I couldn't very well fault him for not having the tools to care for me." John's words came from a deep contemplation that happens over a lifetime.

"I'm glad I didn't know earlier that nursing me is what killed my mother," he explained. "I think I probably could have been an alcoholic had I known it earlier, so when I realized it I just took responsibility for what I could take responsibility for and I moved beyond being a victim of my life circumstances." An expression of gratitude had formed on his face.

"I look forward to meeting her. She'll be the judge, she'll be one measure of the success of my life. You know, that has meant a lot to me, and it's always impacted me. For instance, it was always difficult for me to criticize the poor. I would get mad at the poor, or rather mad at a society's indifference to the poor. No, I didn't grow up being conscious of the effect my mother's death had on me, but I bet you I grew up with it in my subconscious and that helped to guide me."

As noted, after John's mother died, his father took John to live with his mother, John's grandmother. I was curious to know more about his father and the effects he had on John's life. "As a kid, did you ever see your father after he dropped you off at your grandmother's?" I asked.

"He came to see me when I was about three or four. I knew he was coming. When he arrived, I was asleep in bed. He came in the night and took me out in the front of the house by the fireplace. I remember it was somewhat embarrassing. He called me his baby and at that age I was too big to be a baby. But it felt like I belonged to him." He closed his eyes as he spoke as if trying to savor the memory.

"That was my first memory of deep embrace and longing being fulfilled."

I know that the "father wound" can be one of the most painful for children, grown or not, to bear, whether or not the father's absence is justified, or even if the father is absent at all. After all, some people carrying around the biggest baggage related to their fathers comes from the damage their fathers inflicted while they were present. Fatherhood, like motherhood, is a high calling to bear.

John had shared some of these stories about his parents publicly before, and yet he was choosing to be very transparent with me about the details. I had a sense of breathing rarefied air in the room as we talked. I said, "I know that in the house you grew up in, some of your cousins there had their parents around but you didn't have anyone of your own that you belonged to or that belonged to you. For your dad to call you 'baby,' his baby, that had to be meaningful. He belonged to you and you belonged to him."

"Yeah," John nodded. "They say that love is being a part of someone. That I alone am important to someone. That's what thrills me about one of my great-grandchildren. At my house when she comes to find me on the six or seven acres where I am, it's just sort of like tradition that I stop doing what I'm doing and walk back to the house with her. It makes her feel like I belong to her. And I have her by myself. I'm hers. You know it happened to me the other day." He sat back in his chair.

"My great-granddaughter was over and everyone was sitting at the table and I wanted to talk to the group and when I came to the table and sat in the corner, she said, 'You belong here!' The idea was 'you belong to me, and you sit right here.' That just struck me that that's what love is, belonging to someone."

I've found that something happens as you grow older, you see yourself as someone else in the stories you hear. What I mean is, maybe you're watching a movie you've seen a million times before, one that you watched when you were much younger, only now when you watch it you don't identify with the child or teenager relating to their parents as you did before, now you identify with the parent and your empathy lies primarily with them. At some point, John knew that the love he needed from his parents was the same love he got to give his children and then grandchildren and great-grandchildren, and I like to think of the bit of redemption that it brought to the world.

You might be tempted to think John's father chose not to be present and made that choice out of convenience, but remember, this was during the Depression, when men of all races left their families either to find work or because of the shame of not being able to provide for them.

John's father was a real human with his own reasons for doing things. He can't be pigeonholed into a stereotype, especially one that's based on bad information. Someone once wrote that John's father abandoned him, but from what I can tell nothing could be further from the truth. Most people rightly recognize that a mother giving a child up for adoption is a selfless and loving act. Why should we see John's father in any other light?

When I picture John's father getting his three-year-old son out of bed in the middle of the night, cradling him in his arms, the same way I cradle my children, and calling him his baby, it's obvious that his father wasn't lacking in love for his son in the least. I can see them now, faces aglow from the light of the fireplace. John wouldn't have really known or recognized his father, but he knew he belonged to him. I can't imagine the feeling of being held by a parent for the first time while being conscious of it. It's a moving scene. One thing I'm sure of, that father loved his son.

Where We Came From

Before I met John, I would have told you that people are born into the world with a fresh start, a blank page onto which an individual and they alone start writing chapter 1. What I heard in John's stories about his upbringing was that my story didn't start with me. Your story didn't start with you either. To begin with, it took two people to create you and you carry their DNA, so you in a real way carry a part of their story inside of you. Their story didn't begin solely with themselves either. There's a lineage, a legacy. You likely inherited not only genetic traits. In a million small and a few large ways, you absorbed their thoughts and feelings about the world. Those thoughts and feelings were shaped over time by social conditions, family values, and cultural waters. These influences from outside forces don't ask for your permission before impacting you. We don't so much write our own story as we're born into one.

That might sound like fatalism, like we'll be who we'll be and there's not much we can do about it. Maybe you or people you know have even said as much. However, I believe God has given us the ability to resist simply living a story that was handed to us with no revisions and corrections. It doesn't happen by accident, though; it has to be done on purpose.

To be a part of a story that's life-giving, that honors God, we first have to be aware of our story that has been written so far. I realized that day that emotionally healthy people know their stories well, and that is why John is so familiar with his story. Knowing your own story may seem easy, like it happens automatically, but it's remarkable how many people are not in touch with their own past and how it has shaped and continues to shape them. For many of us our past, our relationships, our hardships, wounds, and mistakes go unexamined, and as a result, they control us. John knows this and so he's vigilantly examined his own story.

Despite what some well-meaning church people might say, finding God and praying to receive Christ as your Lord and Savior isn't a cure-all. At least it's not if it stops there. Real encounters with Christ should prompt us to do the difficult work of unpacking the lies we've believed and allow God to search within us to untangle all that mess that's been made in us.

When we think of making a difference in the world, we might immediately think of performing heroic and selfless acts. People like Martin Luther King, Jr., Dorothy Day, and Sojourner Truth come to mind. What we might not realize is that the decision to act in selflessness does not get made in the moment. The heroic actions we read about in books are only a portion of the iceberg peeking above the water. All the while there is a mass several times the size of the visible portion underneath it that allows it to buoy above the waves.

Character, self-sacrifice, compassion, and self-giving love don't come out of nowhere. They are practiced and rehearsed just like any skill or ability. They're also lived out by people who have done deep introspective work. Before we can battle with the demons and injustices in the world, we have to do work with them inside of ourselves.

By the time our brains were formed enough to allow us to have coherent thoughts, we were already a part of a story that had been going on for quite some time. The person we become is heavily influenced by what those in the therapy world call our "family of origin," our parents, siblings, and others that we grew up surrounded by.

We all have our natural character flaws and many times we can trace those flaws back to our family of origin and the role we took in that family. If you are prone to need to control circumstances around you, maybe you came from a family in which you were given too much responsibility too early, and gaining control over any given situation was a way of achieving some stability. Maybe a parent was absent, and as an older sibling you were forced to care for others and make up the difference for that parent. Maybe a parent overshared their personal struggles with you as a child, which forced you to mentally carry problems way too complex for a child to carry, and as a result, you deal with anxiety as an adult.

Even if we had a wonderful, caring, and nurturing family, no family is perfect, and because of that, we all carry inclinations toward certain character flaws. These inclinations will affect every aspect of our lives if we don't do business with what we're carrying from our family of origin. From our marriages, the people we work with, our children, and those in authority over us, it's all affected by an outlook we were taught and inherited.

It is a prerequisite for making peace in the world to have peace within ourselves, and to have that peace we have to be emotionally healthy people who have appropriately examined why we are the person we've become. We must see our shortcomings for what they are and expose them to the light of day. Emotional health is a must for those desiring to bring peace and transformation to the world.

Every day it seems we hear in the news that some supposed great leader has fallen because of a moral failing. We often then learn that this person had, throughout the years, left a trail of people in their wake who were used and abused, emotionally trashed, and exploited for what they could offer the leader, only to be discarded when they were no longer of use. I don't think these people started their careers intending to inflict hurt and pain on those around them. Many of them most likely had altruistic motives, but they simply hadn't done the interior work to adequately deal with the baggage life had handed them.

What I Learned In the Counselor's Office

Now, I can see, as you probably can, that my anger was really veiled self-righteousness and gracelessness. But I couldn't see that at the time. It took years, but I did eventually realize one day that whatever the reason for my anger, it wasn't allowing me to live the abundant life that Christ had promised. I knew I needed help.

That day my counselor enabled me to begin a long process of healing, and later John showed me what healing might look like. For me, while I experienced much joy, and security, I also experienced disappointment and isolation. Everything from living in football-crazed West Texas but not knowing anything about the game, to always feeling a step behind academically, it all mattered, and had left me with a sense of unworthiness and scarcity. It may seem like a stretch but my past caused me to take offense in the most mundane interactions and tell myself that other people were treated better and the reason for this was that they deserved to be treated better.

It would be nice if that was all sifted through in one session with a counselor, but it wasn't. It took time and in fact I'm still vulnerable to those harmful narratives today. Hearing John's story and seeing how he's examined his past has helped me to further develop tools to sit with the Holy Spirit and appraise the stories I tell myself, so I'm able to tell the truth from a lie.

My Problem with Being Human

I worked at Starbucks once. I think everyone should work in the service industry at least once in their life. It can be very humbling. At best, a rare customer will remember a worker's name, smile when they see them, and treat them like a friend. At worst service workers are demeaned, yelled at, and belittled. But on the average, people in the service industry are treated as machines whose purpose is to serve someone. It can be a very dehumanizing experience.

Pastors and people in their "church clothes" were rude to us. People ordered the wrong drink, insisted they didn't, then demanded we make the "right" one.

There were a certain husband and wife who would come into our store and order a very unusual and somewhat bizarre concoction of espresso, flavored syrup, chocolate, and added sweetener. I've long forgotten the recipe, with its specific measurements and instructions. They were indignant when a barista would ask them to repeat one step involved in making the drink. One time the wife looked at those of us behind the counter and condescendingly pronounced: "It's like the blind leading the blind here!" After that, I made it a point to memorize the drink. Whenever they came in, I stopped whatever I was doing and made the drink to save someone the humiliation and to get that couple out of the store as soon as possible.

Often after taking abuse from an angry and entitled customer, I would think to myself, "This job will cause me to lose my faith in humanity." And then immediately after I would think, "Why is my faith in humanity?" I thought that was a particularly spiritual thing to think and I would pat myself on the back for having such a deep and rich thought. Surely the world was lucky to have such a theologian in its midst.

Maybe you're sensing my sarcasm and maybe you agree with my former self. Isn't faith in anything but God wrong? Well, yes and no. We have a non-idolatrous faith in things all the time. We have faith that our cars will get us to work. We, hopefully, have faith in our spouse that they will be faithful to us.

See, I used to think being human was bad. I thought the point of Christianity was to be less human. Humanity was sinful so logically being less human was good. These beliefs made me a frustrated and frustrating person. I found that I couldn't sufficiently hate my humanness to bring about any real change in my life. I couldn't kick any bad habits. I couldn't love people better, and certain people I had a hard time loving at all. Little did I know that John's story would so rearrange the way I saw myself and humanity.

John Shares: Who He Came From

John's journey took on a new trajectory when he moved to California. His son, Spencer, had been going to a Good News Club, a Bible study for children, and invited him to come along. John joined him and was intrigued enough from what he heard to attend the church on Sundays. One Sunday he heard a sermon that changed his life.

I knew that this part of John's story was a real turning point in his life and if I was going to make sense of the questions I was having, I sensed that this was a good place to start.

"Dr. Perkins, I know when you decided to be a Christian you were in church in Southern California one Sunday and heard a sermon on Galatians 2:20." I forced myself to look him in the eyes as I prepared to ask my question. "What exactly happened that day?"

"Oh, yes," he didn't skip a beat, "that was to me the biblical expression of the power of the gospel. It's the good news, the fulfillment of your longing. That day in that church the theology of the church all came out."

This is a theme I would eventually pick up on in John's teachings. He sees the gospel as the fundamental answer, although not the easy self-help answer some try to make it, to the longing of human beings. John also sees the church as the primary deliverer of the gospel. Part of the job of Christians is to draw attention to that need, especially in a culture that tries to distract from that longing at all costs.

"It's difficult to convey how significant it was for me to understand that verse." He thought it over for a second.

"It became my life verse because I *had* been crucified with Christ, and I no longer lived, but Christ lives in me. The life that I now live in the flesh I live in the faith of the Son of God who loved me and gave himself for me." I could tell that he had really located himself within the story of God.

"That day I really believed that he loved me. If there's a God who loves me enough to give his only begotten Son then that really is good news. Spencer, my son, died in 1998, but I wouldn't give him up for anybody." His voice rose and strained briefly.

"But this God was willing to give his son for me! I had heard before that Jesus had died, but never that he had died for me."

I looked up slightly above him as I thought aloud about what he just said. "You realized for the first time that what Jesus was doing on the cross was for your sake."

He nodded. "That he died for me. I had heard he died for the world. He died for those religious people, but until now I had felt no significance in the idea that he had died for me." He looked me straight in the eye.

"Okay, then" I mumbled, trying to figure out how to phrase the question that he just raised in my mind. "I think what I want to know is: How did that change things for you? I see people all the time who've prayed a prayer, they say they're Christians but I can't tell that that's made any change in their life."

He got a very serious look on his face. "Shane, look, I don't know if I became 'born again' at that moment. What I know is that at that moment, I said I want to come to know that God. And in the process of time, I came to know this wonderful wonderful God and then I was born again. We see that we're broken, and when we know Christ we can give that brokenness to him. I watch people live their whole lives in brokenness. I meet people who never get well. They'll be sick all their life. I didn't learn any of this because I was so brilliant. I learned it because I was awakened to my God-given dignity as a human being.

"He saves us from our sin and the wounds and damage of sin, and that for me turned into gratitude. We love him because he first loves us, and that's where my energy comes from. Before, I didn't have purpose."

Who We Came From

To be honest, sitting there with John in that moment, I thought his story was great, but I didn't think it had much to offer me. But I found as time went by I thought about his words more and more. I thought about when he said, "I was awakened to my God-given dignity as a human being." I remembered that the Genesis account tells us that humans bear the image of God. We're all image-bearers. It shouldn't have surprised me that for a correct view of humanity, a Christian should start with Scripture.

> Then God said, "Let us make humankind in our image, according to our likeness; and let them have dominion over the fish of the sea, and over the birds of the air, and over the cattle, and over all the wild animals of the earth, and over every creeping thing that creeps upon the earth."
>
> So God created humankind in his image,
>   in the image of God he created them;
>   male and female he created them.
>
> God blessed them, and God said to them, "Be fruitful and multiply, and fill the earth and subdue it; and have dominion over the fish of the sea and over the birds of the air and over every living thing that moves upon the earth." God said, "See, I have given you every plant yielding seed that is upon the face of all the earth, and every tree with seed in its fruit; you shall have them for food. And to every beast of the earth, and to every bird of

the air, and to everything that creeps on the earth, everything that has the breath of life, I have given every green
plant for food." And it was so. God saw everything that
he had made, and indeed, it was very good. And there
was evening and there was morning, the sixth day.[3]

God made people along with the rest of creation and declared
that they are good. That's no small thing. Remember . . . in the
beginning . . . God created us, as *good*.

We know the rest of the story too. The humans rebelled
against God and his good creation and in a very real way rebelled
against themselves. They were fractured from the inside out, and
so was the world. Then, much later, a new human came along, no
not just a new human but a new kind of human.

Jesus is God to be sure (at least that's what we Christians believe), but he also took on flesh and became human. Yes, he was
born of a virgin, suffered under Pontius Pilate, died on the cross,
and rose again on the third day, but in between all of that, the Gospels of Matthew, Mark, Luke, and John devote a good amount of
space to how Jesus lived his life.

Jesus was a Jewish man, and although the content of his teachings was revolutionary, he taught in the mode of Jewish teachers
of his day, using stories and riddles to make his point. It can sometimes be difficult for modern readers to understand what Jesus was
conveying, but his teachings were unlike anything the world had
ever seen. Even today the teachings of Jesus seem counterintuitive.
"Love your enemies . . . pray for those who persecute you . . . if
anyone steals from you, don't demand anything back . . . blessed
are those who are meek . . ." and on and on. But I don't think Jesus
was only a messenger passing along alien information. He was
in a very real sense showing us how to be human. He was telling
us what it meant to be human, and how to get things back to the
way God intended in the garden before sin corrupted everything.
Jesus, in addition to being God, was the most human human the
world had ever seen. Because remember, humans were created as
good.

3. Genesis 1:26–31.

So what does this have to do with being a peacemaker and being an agent of transformation in the world? Before anyone can be a part of these wonderful life-giving processes, they must experience them for themselves, in themselves, and between themselves and God. And as long as we believe that we're fundamentally broken by design we'll never experience wholeness.

As John told me once "The purpose of humankind is to know God." Everything hangs on that, and if the lens through which we see this God is skewed, everything else will be too. As John shares in the following pages about how he came to know God, pay attention to the main attributes of this God.

Dealing With Our Past

In the following chapters, we'll dive into what being a peacemaker and reconciler looks like. This journey includes, amongst other ideas, radical forgiveness and self-giving love, actions near impossible to sustain when we're carrying around self-destructive narratives and ideas that we've picked up from our past.

Those serious about this work need to ask themselves some serious questions, like: Have I seen any negative patterns in my friendships, romantic relationships, and coworkers? Do those close to me often give me similar feedback about the way I'm being perceived by those around me? If I'm provoking the same negative reaction from those I interact with, is it bad luck or am I the common factor in these situations?

For most of us overcoming our deep-seated flaws will require some level of professional counseling. We can over-spiritualize it, and claim that all we need is to read our Bible and pray more to get the better of our flaws, but that is often a veiled excuse by those not wanting to do the work. Prayer and Scripture are indispensable for this life we're talking about, but they are not a substitute for good counseling, in the same way that when you are physically ill, prayer should be a given, but it doesn't replace going to a doctor and taking medication.

What's At Stake

It would be nice if dealing with our past was only for the big "change-makers," those working for peace on an international scale, or attempting to forgive those who've perpetrated grand transgressions. If that were true then none of this would apply to me. I don't run an international NGO, and I've never been wronged on the scale that we read about in books. I'm just average. On a normal day, I'm just try to get my kids to school on time, try to be good to my next-door neighbors, spend time with my wife, contribute something to my church family, and get dinner on the table. So for most of us, our peacemaking, our reconciliation process, will be on the (seemingly) small scale.

You're trying to make breakfast for your kids, you haven't had coffee yet, your head is pounding because you didn't sleep well the night before, the kids are yelling at each other, and you're tempted to snap, yell at them, and implement some quiet time through intimidation, guilt, and anger.

You're hurt by the actions of a friend, and as a result, you avoid them, telling yourself that they don't really value your friendship, and thus you should give up on it.

Your spouse doesn't seem to do their fair share of the housework, they don't show interest in the things you care about, and you feel distant. You don't bring any of this up, but you harbor resentment as time goes on, resentment that turns to bitterness. Years later the marriage feels lifeless. You've grown apart.

Those of us with "ordinary" lives need emotional health as much as anyone else if we are to be peacemakers where we are. Life is too short for the misery that comes from a life of resentment, suppressed feelings, and stifled relationships. God created us to be known, really known, by ourselves and by others.

Our peacemaking will be a sham if it's extended to everyone but those who know us best, those who live in our homes and eat at our tables. It does no help to the world to perform outward acts of "service," but sow seeds of anger, insecurity, and shame upon those closest to us.

Going Deeper

1. How have you seen the impact of your family of origin play out between you and your coworkers, friendships, marriage, children, etc.?

2. What do you think God might be saying to you about your past?

3. Who are some people that can or have helped you process who you are as a result of your family of origin, like a trusted friend, a counselor, a church small group?

4. What practices would you like to start to utilize to increase your emotional health? (Such as practicing Sabbath, daily prayer meditations, reading Scripture.)

Further Reading

- *Emotionally Healthy Spirituality: It's Impossible to Be Spiritually Mature, While Remaining Emotionally Immature*, by Peter Scazzero

- *Flee, Be Silent, Pray: Ancient Prayers for Anxious Christians*, by Ed Cyzewski

- *The Divine Hours*, by Phyllis Tickle

- *The Divine Conspiracy*, by Dallas Willard

CHAPTER 2

Affirm Dignity

Clyde and His Legacy

M Y CO-PASTOR, APRIL, AND I had just finished leading our
church through a three-week series on what the Bible and
Jesus had to teach us about racial justice and what that might mean
for us as a predominantly white church. I was convinced that it
meant we needed to make some fairly large changes to be a place
welcoming to people of color. I was in charge of creating an out-
line for the series and, truth be told, I was really nervous about it.
Everything that needs to be said about racial justice through the
lens of Jesus can't be said in three weeks (or thirty weeks for that
matter) and I was afraid of not doing it justice and being canceled
by someone in our congregation or listening to our liturgy online.
We did the best we could to talk about privilege, white supremacy,
and ways that our church specifically had fallen short. A friend of
mine who was a Christian woman of color came and spoke with
us on the last Sunday in the series about her experiences in the
church and what steps forward we should take.

In the end, although it was imperfect, there was a sense that
God was really using that series to transform us. I was excited
about our church's future, but still nervous that someone out there
was secretly angry, specifically at me, for not saying more, or failing to say something in the best way. So when a member of our

church called and asked to meet up and talk about the series, I was a little worried. He and I had spent plenty of time together but never one on one and he'd never asked for a special meeting. To my delight he wasn't mad at all, but just wanted to process with me what we had been talking about as a church. Sitting there in a booth at the brewery, he confessed, "What I really have a hard time with is people who don't get it. People who don't think racism is real. People who are racist but think they're not. I have a hard time loving them and being patient."

In that moment I realized that he had just given words to something I had been struggling with too. Since waking up to the reality of what life is like for people of color, and my responsibility as a follower of Jesus to partner with God in bringing about justice and renewal, I've done my best to live out faithfulness, and I've found that many people do not tolerate that message. Dear mentors that discipled me when I was young have decided that I'm now a radical liberal. I've seen people who profess first to be a Christian on their Twitter profiles become hostile and mean as if to claim that white people in America do indeed have privilege is tantamount to blasphemy against the Holy Spirit. And what I really want to do is to say, "Go screw yourself! You're a garbage human being!" I would write them off as moral monsters. But I can't. I can't because once I do that I'm giving in to the same dehumanization that drives racism. It's a failure to see the image of God in everyone. I'm not saying these are moral equivalencies. I'm simply saying they are both manifestations of dehumanization.

Dehumanization: The Common Ingredient

All great human-made atrocities have one thing in common. Slavery, genocide, apartheid, they all start with and are fueled by dehumanization—the refusal to see the dignity of a people group. Looking back at slavery in the United States, one of the most glaring questions is how people could treat another human being so monstrously. If you pay attention, you'll find all sorts of pseudoscience, crackpot philosophy, and dangerous theology that enabled slavery to function and flourish by dehumanizing Black people, because it was only by dehumanizing them that people could inflict horrific mental, physical, and psychological torture on enslaved people. The God-given empathy inside of most people is such that it makes it difficult to inflict much pain on others without first seeing them as less than human beings. That's why dehumanization is a foundational ingredient in cruelty towards a people group.

History is full of those in power dehumanizing people groups, paving the way for oppression. In Nazi Germany in the lead-up to the Holocaust, Jews were referred to as parasites or rats. Sometimes they eventually just got to the point and used the word "Untermensch," which literally translates to "underman," "sub-man," or "subhuman."

Many white people in America during slavery believed that God had created Black people ontologically inferior to whites. They were seen in effect as something closer to an animal than a human; they were "de-humanized." Caricatures of Black people as animalistic, wild, and undomesticated were commonplace. In 1915, fifty-two years after the signing of the Emancipation Proclamation, the movie *The Birth of a Nation* debuted. In it, white men in blackface played the parts of Black men, portraying them as sexually aggressive towards white women, and unintelligent savages. By contrast, the Klu Klux Klan were the good guys, a group of heroes. The film was a hit in its time and many see it as being responsible for resurrecting the Klan just months after its debut. The message of the film wasn't just to say that Black people were bad and white people were good. It was a part of a larger narrative that white people were smart and civilized, separate from animals, while Black people were not. Once Black folks were stripped of dignity in the minds of whites, the oppression could go untethered and unexamined. That's all it took. It was in this kind of culture of dehumanization of Black folks that it was possible for John's older brother Clyde to be murdered by law enforcement.

John Shares: What Happened to Clyde

After that day John and I talked in his hotel room he went back to Mississippi, but we made a plan to talk by phone on a regular basis. One day in May I was sitting in my office at home and I knew I needed to ask John about something I read in one of his books.

Six months or so after returning from World War II as a decorated soldier, John's brother Clyde was killed by local law enforcement, shot down in an altercation after a marshal told him and those he was with, "You [N-word] quiet down."[1]

The N-word has been a tool of ultimate verbal dehumanization towards Black folks since the eighteenth century and it was indispensable in slavery and the Jim Crow era to pave the way for abuse and oppression. It should be no surprise that in this case, it was the precursor to what would happen next.

"I heard that Clyde died in your arms, while your uncle was trying to find a hospital," I said to John that day.

"Yeah, he was taking us to the hospital, fifty to sixty miles, from Mendenhall to Jackson."

"What did that experience do to you?"

"That did a lot of things to me. They first took Clyde to a room nearby with a doctor. When I walked in that room there were Blacks all around and they knew that my brother had been killed. The man that shot him and the sheriff were there along with another white person. I think they thought they had it under control in that room, but they didn't have my pain and my anger under control, and if I would have had a gun I would have shot them. After that, if I was in the streets with other Black people in the town and a white person would walk by, the Black people around me would disperse. They didn't want white people to see them with me because there were afraid that white people would think we were plotting together. It was around that time that I began to see the damage that was happening to us as Black people."

I wasn't exactly sure I understood. "What do you mean by *damage*?"

1. Perkins, *Let Justice Roll Down*, 19.

"Malcolm X said that there were two groups of people," John said. "The house negro and the field negro. The field negro did the hard work and was a slave. The house negro was patronized and he loved his boss more than he loved himself because he got a little more privilege that the other Blacks. I saw that in some Blacks and I knew it was psychological damage. It wasn't just a self-hatred that affected someone internally, but it compelled them to actually protect the system that was enslaving them. I saw that as a sickness. God has ordered my life by giving me these insights along the way that help me focus and process that anger in positive ways."

Internalized Racism

What John is referring to is commonly called "internalized racism." Internalized racism, like most racial concepts, is complex. Sociologist Karen Pyke defines it as the "internalization of racial oppression by the racially subordinated."[2]

In essence, internalized racism happens when the denial of dignity that people of color are bombarded with starts to seep into their own minds and hearts, to the point that they begin to believe the lies. That's what John and Malcolm X were referring to. In a way it's easy to understand. If you grew up in a world that said in a million small and large ways, "you are inferior, untrustworthy, lazy, and less intelligent," you would start to believe that there might be some truth to those claims.

Some media outlets make a cottage industry out of exploiting internalized racism. When a news channel wants to promote a racist bill in congress or justify the murder of an unarmed Black man at the hands of law enforcement, they bring out their token Black commentators to say that the law is in fact "just" in their eyes, or that the Black victim was "acting suspicious," was "somewhere he shouldn't have been, at a time when he shouldn't have been there," or because he had committed some minor crime beforehand, the shooting was justified, and if he had only complied, the police

2. Pyke, "What is Internalized Racial Oppression."

would have done their job by the book and peacefully arrested him. This is, of course, what leads many white viewers at home to feel justified in their opinions. Then the scam is complete.

John explained to me that seeing internalized dehumanization for what it is produces anger, but that anger doesn't have to be a bad thing. "Now I try to harness that anger within the church. I harness that anger by investing my resources in something that has meaning. So now when I think about the poor Black person I remember that they have a good mind, but their mind hasn't been given the opportunities it needs because of a lack of education and exposure and opportunity. After Clyde was shot, I had to live with a deep pain in my gut all the time, a deep pain as I walked around in society. What you do with your time determines your future. What you did with yesterday has a lot to do with today and what do with today has a whole lot to do with tomorrow. Clyde's murder, poverty, and racism, they all come from the same pain and thoughtlessness. We live for survival and we can't see that, and not seeing it perpetuates the problem."

John and Shane Explore the Church's Complicity

Unfortunately, the church has a sad history of dehumanizing too.

"Dr. Perkins, the church you encountered when you were young and the church today . . . How do you explain why at least the white church got it so wrong during those days?"

John answered, "You've got to know the culture of that day and the culture of any day. People become accepting of their culture. The roots of that culture could date back to the Nat Turner uprising. In 1831 Nat Turner led a slave rebellion. It was ultimately unsuccessful. Many slaves were killed by the state for being a part of the rebellion, and out of retaliation, 100 to 200 slaves were killed that had no part in the rebellion. It all led white folks to take more control over slaves and even over free Blacks. Laws were passed that prohibited Blacks from being educated and from gathering together alone. So, even when Blacks went to church there had to be a white minister present. If it wasn't an all-Black church then they would have Blacks in the balcony or a row in the back. That mind-set of needing to control the Black population has had lasting effects."

What was the connection from Nat Turner to the church's complicity in white supremacy and systemic racism? John was revealing something I'd never seen before. The white response to the Nat Turner slave rebellion was one chapter in a legacy of white paranoid dehumanization that took root in the church. A chapter that led directly to withholding valuable educational and societal resources from Black folks. Legacies like that are hard to kill, lasting centuries and generations. The anger of white folks fueled that legacy and continues today.

For Christians, the belief in the *imago Dei* or "image of God" enables us to see past the lie of dehumanization. God made people, *all* people without exception, in his image. This is not new nor is it some liberal spin on Christian theology. It is basic, foundational, historic orthodox Christianity. We can reject racism not because humans decided it was unpalatable at some point (although it most certainly is unpalatable), but because it is Christ himself who showed us the clearest picture of the *imago Dei*.

Dignity Today

The playbook of dehumanization is alive and well today. On June 16, 2015, Donald Trump announced to the world that he was running for president. In that speech, he took the time to focus specifically on people from Mexico.

"When Mexico sends its people, they're not sending their best. They're not sending you. They're not sending you. They're sending people that have lots of problems, and they're bringing those problems with them. They're bringing drugs. They're bringing crime. They're rapists. And some, I assume, are good people."[3]

Never mind that Trump's statements and inferences aren't factually true. A range of sources from fact-checking sites like

---

3. Reilly, "Here Are All the Times."

factcheck.org,[4] to right-leaning think tanks like the Cato Institute, have debunked Trump's claims. The Cato Institute even went so far as to say, "All immigrants have a lower criminal incarceration rate and there are lower crime rates in the neighborhoods where they live, according to the near-unanimous findings of the peer-reviewed evidence."[5]

Notice that, then, candidate Trump tells the gathered crowd the people coming from Mexico are not "you." This is key in de-humanizing a people group. Trump is preempting the human instinct to empathize with other people, to see ourselves in their circumstances. Before our brains can go there, Trump stops us and effectively says, "Nope, they're actually *not* like you."

John says that the root of racism is fear. He told me, "The fear that I think some whites feel now is that America will soon be a country where white people are no longer the majority. That's a truth that is fanning the fear. Donald Trump risked his whole presidential campaign on that fear, along with making 'hate' a value. But God always said, 'Fear not!' So fear is a dangerous thing."

Not Against Flesh and Blood

Many worldviews, even those that seem at odds with each other, operate under the same framework: vanquish your foes, use shame, coercion, and if need be, violence. The wars of the last twenty years show the violence that comes from a hawkish, nationalistic out-look of the world. As I write the debate on gun control rages in the wake of yet another spate of mass shootings. As some politicians call for a ban and even confiscation of military-style weapons, I can think of people by name who swear they will resort to violence before they'll give up their guns.

I have some friends on the left who are quick to call out such violence and idolatrous love of firearms, but some seem to get a

4. Farley, "Is Illegal Immigration?"
5. Nowrasteh, "Illegal Immigrants and Crime."

real thrill out of seeing a video of a Nazi being punched in the face. Some share memes encouraging others to do the same.

Christ-followers are compelled to remember that human enemies are not the ultimate enemies. While other worldviews believe that the key is using the same frameworks of violence, coercion, and shame only "for good," Christians should question the framework itself. Christians believe that evil is not solely or completely embodied in people that can be conquered. Paul in his letter to the church in Ephesus says "our struggle is not against enemies of blood and flesh, but against the rulers, against the authorities, against the cosmic powers of this present darkness, against the spiritual forces of evil in the heavenly places."[6] Therefore we can "defeat" those against us and still lose because we succumb to evil in the form of these frameworks. For Christians, the ends don't justify the means, because the means are a part of the ends.

Although there may be people who choose to be our enemies, we remember that enemy love seems to be what separates a Christ-centered life from almost all other systems of the world. We remember the words of Jesus in his Sermon on the Mount:

> You have heard that it was said, "'You shall love your neighbor and hate your enemy." But I say to you, love your enemies and pray for those who persecute you, so that you may be children of your Father in heaven; for he makes his sun rise on the evil and on the good, and sends rain on the righteous and on the unrighteous. For if you love those who love you, what reward do you have? Do not even the tax collectors do the same? And if you greet only your brothers and sisters, what more are you doing than others? Do not even the Gentiles do the same? Be perfect, therefore, as your heavenly Father is perfect.[7]

It seems that, for Jesus, at no time is a Christian allowed to forget that all people carry the *imago Dei* or image of God, no matter how much they attempt to distort that image.

---

6. Ephesians 2:16.
7. Matthew 5:43–48.

"Love," John told me, "is the antidote. We look to Paul and he says 'Let me show you what never fails, *love*.'[8] How then should we live? Love! Justice comes out of love. Justice is about love. It's because God so loved us, that he doesn't want us to hurt each other."

A Zero-Sum Game

The source of all of this strife is the belief that life is a zero-sum game. That if you're better off then I'm automatically worse off. If you rise out of poverty then I'm poorer because of it. If you achieve a modicum of physical safety then I'm necessarily less safe. There is no "us," there is only "me against you." It is a mind-set and culture of scarcity.

Fortunately, Jesus teaches us a different way to be. Contrary to the fear and scarcity mind-set and culture, Jesus operates out of a mind-set of abundance. In the Gospel of Matthew (as well as the other three Gospels), we're told of a strange happening.

> Now when Jesus heard this, he withdrew from there in a boat to a deserted place by himself. But when the crowds heard it, they followed him on foot from the towns. When he went ashore, he saw a great crowd; and he had compassion for them and cured their sick. When it was evening, the disciples came to him and said, "This is a deserted place, and the hour is now late; send the crowds away so that they may go into the villages and buy food for themselves." Jesus said to them, "They need not go away; you give them something to eat." They replied, "We have nothing here but five loaves and two fish." And he said, "Bring them here to me." Then he ordered the crowds to sit down on the grass. Taking the five loaves and the two fish, he looked up to heaven, and blessed and broke the loaves, and gave them to the disciples, and the disciples gave them to the crowds. And all ate and were filled; and they took up what was left over of the broken

---

8. 1 Corinthians 13:8.

pieces, twelve baskets full. And those who ate were about
five thousand men, besides women and children.[9]

Jesus recognizes a real need of his followers. His disciples let him
know that there's just not enough to feed everyone, however,
Jesus can make enough. These are the economics of King Jesus'
kingdom. There is enough. For everyone . . . enough. No need to
hoard. No need for greed. This is not just about money or food,
although we can trust Jesus for those too. This is about value.
People deny the dignity in others because they doubt their value,
and can't increase that value on their own. They can only make
their value seem greater by making the value of others appear less.
This is why we must derive our value in Christ alone. That's not
some spiritual nicety. We have value simply because we're created
and loved by God; because of whose we are. Therefore we can't
increase our worth by devaluing others. In the kingdom of Jesus,
there is an abundance of worth and value. Like the bread the disciples brought to Jesus, there is always enough to go around. You
have abundant worth and value, and so do I.

Going Deeper

1. What are some ways, small or large, that you've seen dehumanization happen in the media and the world around you?
   What are some ways that you've dehumanized people?

2. How have you seen the zero-sum game played out?

3. How does seeing the *imago Dei* (Image of God) in everyone
   change the way we see others?

9. Matthew 14:13–21.

Further Reading

- *I'm Still Here: Black Dignity in a World Made for Whiteness*, by Austin Channing Brown
- *How to Fix a Broken Record: Thoughts on Vinyl Records, Awkward Relationships, and Learning to Be Myself*, by Amena Brown
- *Be the Bridge: Pursuing God's Heart for Racial Reconciliation*, by Latasha Morrison

CHAPTER 3

It Will Cost You Something

I GREW UP WITH a typical evangelical faith. I walked down an aisle as a kid to tell my pastor that I had prayed to accept Jesus as my Lord and Savior. My parents faithfully took me and my sister to church regularly. When I was a teenager I latched onto my youth minister, who was a gifted teacher and loved all of us in the youth group well. I went on mission trips, helped out at vacation Bible school, and went to youth camp. I had a genuine faith and love for Jesus, but in the day-to-day I just thought that meant waiting until heaven, reading my Bible and praying every day, and trying not to sin too much. Not sinning too much meant not having sex, not smoking, not doing drugs, not watching R-rated movies, and letting my friends know not to cuss around me. It was more of a code of conduct than an embodiment of faithfulness. Furthermore, in the real world the people I thought of as faithful were middle class or wealthier, had good jobs, leaned right politically, and although I didn't realize it then, they were all white. In total, good Christians were respected in their communities and were what we considered productive members of society. I believed that if I continued to be a good Christian, I too would end up being respected and a productive citizen. Of course I would grow up to evangelize too. I would tell people about Jesus so that they could also be respected and productive, and evangelize. In this way, I realize now that my Christianity was one big pyramid scheme. You evangelize, which was a fancy word for trying to pursue someone to follow Jesus, and if they asked what it meant to follow Jesus you could say something or other about being good, but most importantly following Jesus meant you tried to pursue other people to follow Jesus, and on and on.

I won't go into detail about how that all changed for me, but suffice it to say, as I got older my mental house of faith developed some cracks in the walls. I always knew that I had found something real in Jesus that was worth holding on to, but I knew there were some major incongruity between the Jesus revealed in Scripture and the Jesus I had known. I was lucky enough that I was led through my times of deconstruction by other Christians and not people who wanted me to give my faith up altogether.

It's not like I got *everything* wrong in my younger days. Doing harmful things to my body, not taking in every bit of media indiscriminately, and adopting societal mores around sex aren't embodying faithfulness, but my problem was thinking that faithfulness stopped there (in addition to some legalism, and judgmentalism that came with that code of conduct). I came to see God's great love for the poor, outcast, and marginalized. I saw that following Jesus had massive and total claims over how my family spent our money, where we lived, where our kids went to school, if and how we voted, and the way we treated the earth. God was not giving up some of his desires because it sounded too liberal or too conservative and neither could I.

What I was learning is that real Christianity is costly. Jesus was clear about as much when he said "Whoever comes to me and does not hate father and mother, wife and children, brothers and sisters, yes, and even life itself, cannot be my disciple . . ."[1], ". . . I am sending you out like sheep into the midst of wolves . . ."[2] And "You will be hated by all because of my name . . . ,"[3] just to name a few instances. It seems that if you're doing Christianity right, there will be sacrifices, you'll lose some friends, and some people just

1. Luke 14:26.
2. Matthew 10:16.
3. Matthew 10:22.

won't like you. I have to be honest. I hate that. I don't like it when people don't like me. I don't like it when people are angry at me. I'd rather be everyone's best friend. In short, I'm not at peace with what I've learned it means to be faithful to this Christ King. Maybe I shouldn't be. But, when faced with heartbreaking challenges I know the best thing I can do is turn to people who are older, wiser, and have experience with or beyond what I'm going through. I knew the tribulations John had been through made mine look like a cakewalk, but it's that reason why he's the perfect mentor. If you want to run a 5K and you're friends with someone who's climbed Mount Everest, that's the person you need to listen to.

John Shares: The Cost of Engaging in the Fight for Civil Rights

John's story is most prominently characterized by love, but it's not a cheap, easy love. It's not a love conceived of by people who write greeting cards or romantic comedies. It's a durable love that withstood years of self-giving.

In early spring I was at my desk in what was part office for me and part nursery for our daughter, or as we called it the "nurffice." My desk was against the back wall where there was a large picture window. I was catching up with John on the phone and facing the bright sunlight. The view wasn't much. In fact it was just about four feet away from my neighbor's fence, but the bright sun was shining down and there was a very small tree in between with a few anemic branches sprouting new green leaves.

"Dr. Perkins, after Clyde died, I know you moved to California. What was your time there like? I know you were on your way to building a good and somewhat comfortable life for yourself there. You married Vera Mae, you started a family, and had a big house. You were moving up in your job at a supermarket."

"Yes, that company exploded," he said. "I started as a janitor and I got to know the people. I could have been a supervisor, but it was still somewhat segregated. This company was run by a Catholic family, a good one, people who believed in their faith, and if you didn't steal and if you didn't skip out on the job, they might transfer you [if you performed poorly], but they wouldn't fire you."

I got the feeling that even this modest level of opportunity was rare in the South. John worked hard, he was able to buy a house, he married Vera Mae, and they started a family together. After his son Spencer introduced him to his Bible study, and John became a Christian, things began to change.

"It seems like things were going well for you, so how did you wind up back in Mississippi?" I asked, a little confounded.

"Well, I remember God began to lead us," he said as if trying to remember the sequence of events. "I was going to prison camps with these business friends of mine from the Christian Business Men's Club. It was almost all white men in the club. I was the first Black man to join, and they absolutely received me."

"What year was this?" I interrupted.

"This was 1957. A group of them went to prison camp schools in the mountains there in San Dimas, California, not far from where we lived. The inmates were juveniles on work details. I thought I was going to see some old men the first time I went. They took me because they had heard my testimony and wanted me to give it there, so I did that the first morning. I had never assumed that it was going to be a majority of Black people." I heard the sadness in his voice.

"I heard them talk, I saw that they talked just like me, in Ebonics. They or their parents had migrated from Mississippi or somewhere thereabouts. Here I was, feeling significant. I had a big house. I'm feeling good about myself. I had Jesus, and I'm beginning to be accepted by others around me. These businessmen owned the town and they were my friends and here were these boys, trapped. I can remember being in their shoes back in Mississippi and hearing a gospel that didn't connect to me. I had heard about God. I had heard some people preach but I hadn't heard the central message. I had heard churches talk about God, sing their sermon, hoot and holler. I had seen people falling on the floor, and shouting out. But I never connected that with anything worthwhile. I will say, amid the shouting you sensed a struggle. I understand that it came out of a struggle, but it was difficult for me to identify."

Although he didn't know it then, this was the genesis of John's public ministry. As he spoke I could tell that he could still go back to that first trip to the prison camp and see the faces of those young men.

"So," I began thinking out loud. "You had a desire to reach people that were like you were when you were young?"

"Right, my own folk. It reminded me of Romans 10, where Paul says his heart's desire was for the Jewish people to be saved, even while he was called to reach the Gentiles. His vision was that if the Jewish people were redeemed they would carry out their original message of winning all people to Jesus Christ, that's what he thought. He said 'my heart's desire, and prayer to God,' . . . 'for I bear them record that they have a zeal of God'[4] and 'they have a zeal for God but it's not according to the word of knowledge.'"[5]

"These religious people I remembered back in Mississippi had a zeal but the way they expressed it wasn't relevant to the poverty and the pain we experienced, and many are still experiencing, every day. I'm not looking down on their worship. I know there was a purpose and reason for their style, it was therapeutic for Black folks living in society. It just didn't do anything for *me*. Today some churches believe that what they're doing on a Sunday morning is more important, but Sunday morning should equip you to do work 'out here.'"

John's words were convicting. How many churches spend a disproportionate amount of their resources on a Sunday morning gathering, and make it the centerpiece of their existence? Many don't even use that time to equip people for any work outside the church walls. Much of what constitutes as "church" today is designed to make us comfortable and accommodates an American lifestyle, convenient and effortless.

"So what it seems like what you're saying is, that what you saw in the gospel in California was something that changed people

4. Romans 10:2.
5. Romans 10:2.

and had an effect on their lives. It wasn't escape from life, it was changing life?," I tried to clarify.

"Right, that's right!" he replied.

It's easy to underestimate how leaving California in the late 1950s to go back to Mississippi was an enormous sacrifice for a Black man and his family. California, though far from providing true equality, as nowhere today provides true equality, sounds far ahead of Mississippi at the time. California had afforded John the ability to earn and buy a house, provide for his family, and obtain a modicum of the stability that we all want. Now, he was leaving all of that behind so that he could minister to those who needed it most in Mississippi. I saw this as one of John's first sacrifices for following Jesus. It gave me confidence that John's life would give me direction to deal with understanding the ways in which the real gospel had caused me to lose out on the life I wanted for myself, one that didn't cause a commotion or laid claim to my comfort.

John moved back to Mississippi at the beginning of 1960, and at that time two churches and one club made up of Black Christians that he had built connections with in California were supporting him in his ministry.

Every year, once John and his small group had their summer ministry off to a start, he would go back to California to raise money. In the early days, he and Vera Mae would take the children, stay a couple of weeks, and while his family spent time with their friends, John would find any kind of Christian meeting—a women's meeting, some kind of meeting in the Black community, and one in the white community—and they would take up an offering. John went back every summer to raise enough money for the winter, but that grew over a ten-year period. Eventually, John had 2,000 people on his mailing list and around 900 people that would contribute. Most gifts were between $2 to $50. Some folks would give annually and some monthly. Some churches would give $50 a month, which John considered a strong gift, and if a church was giving $200 a month, that was considered big money back then.

"Dr. Perkins, When you went back to Mississippi you first started child evangelism clubs, teaching Bible studies in the Black high schools, and other types of church programs, but then you got involved in the civil rights movement and starting cooperatives and other economic initiatives for Black folks. Was it obvious to you from the beginning that as a Christian you should get involved in civil rights?"

Looking back it seems obvious to most that the civil rights movement was a good thing, a God-ordained movement even. In fact, I've often grieved that more Christians weren't on the front lines. But I was born in the 1980s so I've always had the benefit of hindsight.

John seemed to be trying to figure out where to start to best answer my question. Eventually, he said, "Well, when I first moved back to Mississippi I didn't intend on getting involved in civil rights, I intended on evangelizing. I was so *intent* on trying to spread the gospel. I got there in June, and in the summer in Mississippi, people have all kinds of religious meetings and revivals, because you have a time when all the crops have been planted, and there's not much else you have to do. Back then Sunday was always a day off so many Black people scheduled their activities on Sunday. So I would fill that time with opportunities to spread the gospel. Then in August of that year, I got my children enrolled in school. These were segregated schools. The principal would talk to the parents, and it's a big day when you brought your children back to school. It felt like we were in a church, the way the principal kept using religious talk. I had never been involved in anything like this in Mississippi before. I asked the principal that day if he would like for me to come and talk to the children sometime about Christ and I told him I would teach a Bible study and he said, 'Yeah, that would be great, we have time.' During that time they were building what we thought were nice schools for Blacks, the kind we had never had before. In the old system, one teacher used to teach four to five classes, you know, but now it was organized better, so they had more time and needed something to fill that time. So I came and taught the kids about Jesus. The principal loved it and so he told me about other principals of other schools, many of them his cousins, and they would invite me in for what they called an 'activity time.' I would set up a talk in a school once a month and sometimes twice a month, depending on the size of the school, because at some you couldn't get them all in the gym at the same time. After about two years I was going to fifteen high schools and elementary schools, and two junior colleges."

"Ah, I see where this is going," I interjected.

John explained that this was all happening in the fall of 1960 and soon after the civil rights movement really got started. Medgar Evers was murdered in 1963. Then the civil rights act of 1964 was passed. The civil rights movement really started to spread during the summer of 1964. That's when many civil rights workers, white and Black, began a voter registration drive in Mississippi and campaigned against voter intimidation and suppression. Many of the workers found themselves at the receiving end of violence at the hands of the KKK and law enforcement. In June, Mount Zion Methodist Church in Philadelphia, Mississippi, was burned down and three civil rights workers were murdered after attempting to investigate the arson. In John's community Black people were being stopped and threatened. Many were locked in jail, and would call John and ask him to get them out. The movement really snowballed from there. In 1965 Malcolm X was killed, and in 1968 Martin Luther King, Jr. was killed.

John continued, "When I was going in the schools talking to the kids I would say nothing about civil rights, I would only talk about the Bible and the word of God, otherwise there were Black folks who would have went to the white folks and told them, and they would have pressured me out."

"But I couldn't have a conversation in the Black community without civil rights coming up. It wasn't like I had an option to *join* the movement. You didn't choose it, you were drafted. If you were a leader in the community, they pushed you to one of two sides, 'What side are you on, son?,' and you might respond, 'I'm on the freedom side.' If you weren't on the freedom side you were on the Uncle Tom side. Being called an Uncle Tom back in those days was worse than calling a Black person a nigger. Now you might ask, 'Did everyone pick a side?' No, but those people just accepted life as it was and stepped aside, so to speak. Many Black folks weren't even going to church because they would be ridiculed for not taking a stance and wanted to avoid that. I would say that 75 percent of the Black people wanted to do something about the oppression they were experiencing and were active somehow in the movement."

This wasn't to say John wasn't asked to address current events other than civil rights. "The Black schools invited me in at different times," he said. "Like when Kennedy was killed. When all of that killing was happening they began to invite me in for special days to hold a chapel program. They thought the job of the Christian at that time was to keep the kids under control in school by talking about Jesus, talking about the church and God, not talking about civil rights."

Fearing I knew the answer, I asked, "So did the white evangelicals back in California withdraw support for you when they learned that you were involved in the civil rights movement?"

"Oh yeah," he said. "It began to hit the fan when my white evangelical friends back in California would hear about my involvement and they would come and visit me. About 1967 to 1968, after five or six years of raising support, I lost almost all of my evangelical support. The churches stopped, most of them from California, because of my involvement in the civil rights movement."

I followed up, "It had to be hard for you to do what you knew was right, and also know that you were cutting your own legs out from underneath you by alienating your base of support, your very livelihood."

"Oh yeah," he replied. "You know, the white folks put Black people in one of two categories: the radicals, and the ones who could wait. To most whites, the radicals, the ones who wanted their freedom right now, were evil. That's what makes Martin Luther King, Jr.'s, "I Have a Dream"[6] speech so powerful. He used the words 'the urgency of now.'[7] That's pretty powerful if you think of

6. King, "I Have a Dream."
7. King, "I Have a Dream."

it, 'the urgency of now,' that we can't wait any longer. King called the other way 'gradualism.'"[8]

"Even today white people try to put Black folks in one of two categories. Some of my Black friends talk about the way that white people will sometimes try to figure out what kind of Black person they are. Are they the kind of Black person that will go along with some subtle racism and stereotyping, who will play the game, or are they the 'angry' and 'political' type of Black person who might speak up in those kinds of moments?"

"God provided, though. Somehow I got to know a Southern white gentleman named Mr. Kurt Lamb. He had started talking to me in 1964. So I wrote him one letter and I explained how I lost all of my support."

Kurt Lamb was a well-to-do businessman that loved Christ and loved what John and his ministry were doing. When he was younger, he was a traveling salesman, going after backwoods stores in the Carolinas. That's where he met a Black man who led him to Christ. John figures Kurt, like a lot of people at that time, was probably nice to Black people but as far as segregation was concerned, he accepted that that was the way of the South. But then as Black folks began to get locked in jail and beaten by police for small things, John thinks Kurt began to reconsider, realized it wasn't right, and asked himself what he could do about it. Kurt thought he needed to bring people to Jesus Christ.

After receiving a letter from John, Kurt called him on the phone. He wanted John to come to meet him in Charlotte, North Carolina, where he lived. So John and Vera Mae went to Charlotte. He told John and Vera Mae, 'The work you are doing in sharing Christ amid this crisis is too important. I want you to write down your budget with all of your expenses and I'll take care of it.' And just like that John and Vera Mae had their support back. Mr. Lamb died in the early 1970s and after that his sons-in-law, two preachers who had married his daughters, supported John's family because they loved and respected their father-in-law.

8. King, "I Have a Dream."

There's a myth out there of the white savior. The myth says the plight of Black folks has improved because a few white folks bravely and selflessly stood up for them. White saviors are very popular in Hollywood movies based in the civil rights era, and as a white person, when I see them, I'm lulled into thinking that those stories are real, when they are more often than not works of fiction, or at least embellished beyond recognition. I'm also tempted to think that *I* would be that person courageously defending my Black friends against the forces of "the bad white people," had I been alive in those days. The truth is that if I had been born forty years earlier I would have been brought up in the same cultural waters as all white people during the Jim Crow era. I would have likely been taught, implicitly and explicitly, all of the bigoted things that almost all white people of the day believed.

There are no white saviors. Kurt Lamb must have been a very good man. In fact, to this day John has tremendous gratitude for what Kurt did for him, and he looks back on their relationship as an authentic friendship. John also knows that Kurt was no one's savior. It's admirable that he gave what sounds like a considerable amount of wealth to John and his ministry, but we have to ask why he was able to obtain such wealth when such a feat was virtually unheard of for a Black man or woman in that time. It's not that Kurt's wealth was ill-gotten, but receiving a donation from a white man wouldn't have been necessary had Black men and women had the same opportunities and access that whites did.

John Shares: An Even Greater Cost

At some point in our friendship John asked me to come visit him at his house in Jackson. Our phone calls were wonderful but nothing beats talking face to face. I was delighted at the invitation, so after some planning with my wife, Kate, and arranging our schedules I got on a plane and flew to Jackson for four days. The Perkins's house is in a neighborhood of craftsman-style homes and next door to the headquarters of John and Vera Mae's foundation that helps those in need in Jackson. Over my four-day visit I participated in, or more accurately nodded my way through John's 4 AM men's Bible study in his living room. We made pancakes together in the morning and later picked okra from his garden. He drove me around the neighborhood showing me once dilapidated houses that his nonprofit purchased and remodeled for single mothers to live in affordably. We watched TV together and talked about the news. But mostly we sat at his dining room table where I asked him questions all day.

In our past conversations, John had alluded to what happened in that jail in Brandon, Mississippi in 1970, but we hadn't talked about it directly. I wasn't sure I was ready, but I knew I needed to ask about the day that nearly cost him everything.

"Going back to that night in 1970, I've read what happened, but can you tell it to me in person?" I shifted in my chair uncomfortably.

John answered, "We had been having marches in Mendenhall, demonstrating our desire, our demand, for what we wanted the city to do." His voice was slow and measured. "That night there were some young folks who were going back to Tougaloo College."

These college students had been partnering with John in the marches in Mendenhall. They would load up into a van at Tougaloo College in Jackson, drive to Mendenhall, and then drive home at the end of the day when the marches were over.

This day the students were in two vans, driven by Doug Huemmer and Louise Fox, two white students. Doug in his van was pulled over by the highway patrol on the outskirts of Jackson. While they were pulled over, Louise found a telephone booth, made a call to John and his friends, and told them that Doug's van had been pulled over and they were probably going to be taken to jail in nearby Brandon, Mississippi.

John continued the story, "So me, my friends Rev. Curry Brown, and Jo Paul Buckley, hopped in a van to meet them at the jail. We should have known better. When we got to the jail the highway patrol met us outside."[9]

9. This story is told more exhaustively in John's *Let Justice Roll Down*, and it should be read to appreciate the eerie situation of so many white men in

"You were set up, weren't you?" I wanted to clarify.

"I was either set up or I blindly ran into it," he said quickly, as if he'd thought about it a lot over the years. "They might have said 'lookey here, exactly what we would have wanted to happen. This fool walked right into it.' It was so well calculated that it's easy to believe that it was set up. I didn't think much about that when it was happening, but I can look back and tell you almost exactly how it was planned. They arrested one van of students but didn't even stop the other van so that that group could call us. I didn't realize how deep in it I was at the time with the police watching me so closely and waiting for an opportunity to silence me somehow."

John had brought up something else that might be easy to miss. The antagonism that law enforcement showed John, the same antagonism that had been inflicted on so many Black leaders before, during, and after the Jim Crow era, was often not a mere random act of a few racist individuals gone rogue. It was a part of a complex, systemic, and organized institution bent on criminalizing and dehumanizing Black people. John was being watched by the police before that day. They were plotting against him.

These kinds of tactics were pervasive during that time. Martin Luther King, Jr. had his phone wiretapped by the FBI with the approval of then attorney general Robert Kennedy, and under the leadership of FBI director J. Edgar Hoover. The FBI even attempted to blackmail Dr. King with a threatening letter that Dr. King believed was designed to manipulate him into committing suicide. Taken together, one can see that when someone with a badge acted out violently and unjustly toward black men, it was often not an action perpetrated in the heat of a moment or only the product of individuals' seething racism, but the end product of hours of plotting and systemic organization. It's into this racist state-sponsored system that John and his friends walked that night at the Brandon jail.

---

official state uniforms, patrol cars' blue lights flashing, and a helpless van of college students at their mercy, soon to endure their violence. What happened to John is also told in more detail in the book.

When John, Rev. Brown, and Mr. Buckley got out of their car in the parking lot of the jail, the patrolman met them there, arrested them, and started hitting them.

John remembers, "They might have said 'Now this gives us the opportunity to really torture these people, to teach them a lesson,' and of course you know what torture is . . ." He paused and looked me in the eyes. ". . . it's making someone believe that they're about to be killed. *They* sure knew what torture was."

"When we got inside the jail that's when it really started. All kinds of torture. When you're brought as near to death as you can be, you're first going to tell the truth. Then, as the torture gets worse, you say exactly the words that they put in your mouth, you repeat them because somehow, you think that if you do that, you're going to avoid death. That's the dilemma of torture. Whatever the torturer wants you to say, that's what they'll get." He lightly smacked his open hand on the table. "The tortured do both, they tell the truth, then they say whatever they're told to say."

For John, what they made him say, or in this case read, were the demands that the Black community in Mendenhall had been marching for. One of the deputies or patrolmen had found a copy of the demands, and after beating John half to death they all made him read the demands to them as a kind of performance.

"The uniqueness of the torture . . ." John's voice was quiet. "Shane, I don't describe it that much in my interviews and my writings. I'll just say they want to destroy you sexually."

He went on the explain that there was something in the Southern white man's mind back in those days, a mixture of fear and the belief in the myth of an overactive sex drive in Black men. Poor whites thought Black people had something a little bit beyond human sexuality. That was why they were so intolerant of interracial marriage; white men wanted to protect their white women from being exposed to this hypersexuality. Much of the killing and hanging of Black folks was on the assumption that they had raped or made some kind of unwanted sexual advance toward a white woman. Sometime white mobs even castrated Black men.

"It was the fear of Black folk's sexuality that caused them to do what they tried to do when they were torturing us. That's why, when we were being tortured, we had to turn over, that's why we had to ball up into a knot because they always wanted to kick you in your groin, they wanted to kick us in a way that humiliated us sexually. The idea was that you can't do more than kill a person, but you could torture someone first before killing them. That was the kind of anger with which they attacked us. Usually, when I tell the story . . . ,"—he paused to look at me—"I tell about the beating, but I don't emphasize the fact that they were trying to destroy us sexually. Each one of the people who were tortured during the civil rights movement would say the same thing, they knew how to roll up. They rolled themselves up into a ball to protect their private parts. It's not that balling up stopped all the sexual violence. It was known to happen during that time, that the torturer would put sticks and things up a Black man's rear end, and you can't avoid that, you can't curl up backward, only frontwards. So all we could do was keep rolling on the floor. Try to keep rolling, and they are kicking you, and kicking you in a way to get you out of that ball, so they can kick where they really want to kick you. *That* was the kind of torture that we were being tortured with."

To say I was shaken by what I had just heard would be an understatement. This wasn't in any of John's books. I had to stop and take a few deep breaths while I looked out of the window of John's dining room. Every once in awhile throughout the course of my friendship with John, we would be talking and the reality that I was speaking to the man that I had read about for years would hit me. This was one of those moments. I looked across the table at a man in his eighties, sharing his home, food, and time with me, and thought about how one night he endured ghastly torture at the hands of law enforcement.

After a few moments passed I knew I needed to keep going if I wanted to know the full story. "Did they have weapons?" I asked.

"Yes," he said slowly. "In the middle of kicking me, they were hitting me with their nightsticks, then they put me in this cell. That's when I thought it was sudden death because there were

45

some jailers there with these blackjacks, weapons you put around your hand and its got steel in it, it's wrapped up in leather. What made them such an effective weapon was the way it hit you. It would crush you. They were hitting me with it and it was as if it was paralyzing me. I don't quite remember when it stopped, but I would say it was twenty-five years or more after my Brandon beating, I would be sitting down like normal at my table or eating somewhere, and my head would begin to hurt, just like it did in the middle of my beating." He spread his fingers out and grabbed the sides of his head.

"Sometimes just the memory of getting hit with that blackjack would bring that same pain in my head. That feeling that I had that night when they were taking me up the steps would reappear. The pain would come and it would hang around ten to fifteen seconds in my head and I would just wring my hands over my head and then it would go away. It went on for years until somewhere along the line God took that away from me. I don't get that anymore, but it went on for years. The trauma . . . I know what people who have been to war are talking about when they speak of trauma. I know that trauma. I lived with that trauma."

I asked, "How long did the whole ordeal last? The beating? Did they beat you until the next day?"

"No. It probably lasted from let's say 9 PM probably to 11 PM or some time like that. The thing was, they thought the FBI was coming, so at some point they stopped and made us mop up our blood from the floor. Then, somehow they found out the FBI *wasn't* coming, and so then they tortured us some more. Later we had to clean up the rest of the blood. Finally they threw me in a cell on the second floor, but first they beat me to a pulp as I was going upstairs."

Eventually they threw John in a cell with the college students, who picked John up and put him into a bed. The students took towels and their shirts and soaked them full of water and wrapped them around John's head to try to keep the swelling down and save his life. At some point John passed out. When morning came, John's head and whole body were, in his words, "just dysfunctional."

"That's when Vera Mae and my son came in. They wouldn't let us talk alone. Vera Mae got right up beside me and was trying to talk to me while trying to keep the patrolmen from hearing what we were saying."

I interjected, "I know your friends couldn't get enough collateral to bond you out until around late in the afternoon that day. What kind of state were you in medically when you finally got out?"

"Oh, I went straight to the hospital and the doctor had to draw fluid from my head where they hit me. My head was puffed, there were knots, and it was full of liquid and the doctor had to leach those and draw the liquid out with a syringe and then patch it back. I went back to him in a day or so and he would put new patches on me."

As a new father just initiated into the experience of being responsible for a young life I felt in my heart that the trauma had to have affected not only Vera Mae but John's children too. "What kind of toll did this take on your family?" I asked.

"My son Spencer wrote a book, *More Than Equals*,[10] and in it he says that when he came to see me with Vera Mae in the jail, he could see the 'humiliation,'[11] that I felt for my son to see me in that condition. That was a good description. He expressed words, what I felt, in a way I couldn't express, because that was hard, *hard* . . ." He raised his voice. "My son seeing his daddy beaten into helplessness."

The beating of John and his friends happened on a Saturday night. Another march was scheduled for the next Saturday in Mendenhall and John came. He made a speech right in front of the highway patrol and everyone in attendance. During that speech, Spencer saw his dad and, as John puts it, "was sort of horrified, and saw him as someone who was somewhere between courageous and mad."

Later on, John's daughter came to the hospital after one of his operations to undo the damage done by the beatings. She saw the

10. Perkins and Rice, *More Than Equals*.
11. Perkins and Rice, *More Than Equals*, 46.

tubes and wires attached to him and knew all of that was the result of the beating. She ran out of the hospital screaming. Vera Mae went out and tried to console her. John laid there in his hospital bed feeling helpless. That day his daughter said, "I will never never never never like white folks again, never never!"

This whole business of John's torture; it's dark, it's indefensible. Yet, I know what the average white person would have said in 1970 upon hearing of John's torture. I know because the average white person is still saying the same things today.

"He shouldn't have been tortured but . . ."

"He shouldn't have been antagonizing law enforcement."

"He shouldn't have been marching, disrupting everyone's day, interrupting the flow of traffic."

"He should just put his head down and been a model citizen."

They say:

"There's another side to this story."

"I heard that he had some issues in his past."

John's decision to embody the gospel, to be a part of God's work of justice in the world cost him, and then it cost him some more. It almost cost him his physical life. In one of our conversations John said something that I thought was peculiar. He said he thinks white people might have to go through something similar to what Black folks have had to endure for racial justice to have a chance. It's hard to say what that might be, and it would be unwise to think that any trial white folks could go through would be as difficult as what Black folks have had to endure in my country throughout the centuries. But I think a start might be a loss of status and relationships for white people. If white people turn away from the lies of racism, of American meritocracy, there will be a cost. Friends and family who thought we were the "right kind of people" will think differently of us. We'll lose friends. We'll wonder why we didn't get invited to certain parties and social gatherings. Our businesses might even suffer because of our unpopular opinions in certain circles.

Embodied Gospel, Embodied Liberation

A direct line can be drawn from the day John realized that Christ died for him to his being a leader in the civil rights movement. Deciding to follow Christ isn't about praying magic words and then waiting until we die so that we can go to heaven, and it's not about simply arranging the mental furniture in our minds so that we believe all the right things, although it's often presented that way.

The intricacies of following Christ are difficult to unpack in the space we have here, but two metaphors have helped me. First, following Christ is more akin to making marriage vows. Many a marriage has been doomed because the participants thought that saying their marriage vows was a culmination, a crescendo, that finalizes a journey. In reality, the vows are only the start. Those who have made marriage work over the long haul know that after the vows are said the real work begins, and many of us know of marriages that didn't work out because those involved thought the hard work was over once they said "I do." Second, following Christ is like giving our allegiance to a king. Okay, so talking about following a king is a little antiquated, but we can still get the basic concept. Allegiance to a king is not a onetime event and it's not just mentally agreeing to some truths. It requires something on our part, an ongoing and durable loyalty. For John, as for us, after he "said his vows" and swore his allegiance to the true king, the real work began. The gospel is embodied. If it's not embodied, then it's not the gospel.

When I talk to John about his life and I refer to the sacrifices he made, he gently rebuffs me. One day I mentioned his decision to move back to Mississippi from California as an example and he quickly told me "Don't glorify that!" For him, his choice to go back to Mississippi, minister to the Black folks there, and engage in the fight for civil rights, was a step up in the world, because he was following God's call. In his words it "awoke him to his dignity," and that awoke others to their dignity as well. It occurred to me, for John following the lead of Christ was not seen as some burdensome sacrifice, it was liberation. I've decided that when I'm saddened by the cost of following Christ—lost friends, status, and wealth—I'm going to remember the liberation I've gained, and the joy I've found.

Going Deeper

1. Would you say your faith is a risky faith like John's or a safe faith? What could you do to embrace riskier faith?

2. Can you name a time when your faith cost you something?

Further Reading

- *The Power of Proximity: Moving Beyond Awareness to Action,* by Michelle Ferrigno Warren

- *At Home in Exile: Finding Jesus among My Ancestors and Refugee Neighbors,* by Russell Jeung

- *Adventures in Saying Yes: A Journey From Fear To Faith,* by Carl Medearis

CHAPTER 4

Embracing Forgiveness

Overcoming the Brutality of White Supremacy

"FATHER, FORGIVE THEM; FOR they do not know what they are doing." Those words of Jesus on the cross are among the most famous in the Bible. Earlier in Jesus' life, when teaching his disciples how to pray, he said "For if you forgive others their trespasses, your heavenly Father will also forgive you; but if you do not forgive others, neither will your Father forgive your trespasses." It's obvious from Scripture that a life of following Jesus will be marked by radical forgiveness. It's one thing to know this cognitively. I do know that God wants me to forgive. I believe the cliche that withholding forgiveness is like drinking poison and expecting the offender to die. Still, it's difficult. Once again, John and his life give us a template, a modern example to follow along on the pathway to forgiveness.

John's story could have ended with him being beaten by the police and his family could have learned the lesson that white people aren't to be trusted, and who could have blamed them? They had all suffered so much at the hands of white folks, not just the ones in uniform who beat and tortured John, but the ones who stayed silent, and the ones that stopped supporting their ministry when they learned that John wasn't the kind of Black person they wanted him to be. But the story didn't end there.

John Shares: Healing and Forgiveness

I asked John what happened after that day in the hospital, when his daughter said she would never like white folks again.

He shook his head. "Thank God she overcame that. Thank God! She's lived in a place with whites and Blacks together most of her life now. I think that's what was healing for her and my son Spencer. They had to have some white people that they could talk to, that could endure their anger, still reach out to them, and embrace them."

The Perkins kids seem to find strength and healing within community, I observed.

John responded, "I think that's why Spencer and his family so desperately wanted to live in community with people different from themselves. They didn't want to give up on their Christian faith. They did not want to give up on the Bible. Still, it was difficult for them."

John's son, Spencer, under the influence of his father's life and work, grew up to be committed to racial justice and reconciliation. He along with his partner in ministry, a white man named Chris Rice, began an integrated Christian group home where they lived with their families and others. Culture tells us there are just some groups that can't get along. Maybe no one would say that out loud, but look at our segregated cities, look at the way white people can't fathom the experiences of Black people. But there were Spencer, Chris, and their families, living under the same roof. They were resisting and subverting a sick culture. They said in effect, "actually there *is* a reality where we can be together, and where we should be together; the upside-down kingdom where Jesus Christ rules and reigns."

Mulling it all over, I confessed to John, "I can just imagine that if such a great injustice had happened to me, that I would struggle with anger for a really, really long time." I was angry just from hearing John tell me his story, even though I already knew the gist of it.

He smiled at me sweetly. "But you know there's a story I tell about that. Later on, I went to the hospital with symptoms of a heart attack, and one of the people who treated me was a doctor who wanted to be a nun but took up medicine instead. She had come down to Mississippi during the civil rights movement and had seen the suffering and the pain and she sort of saw herself as a missionary, I'll put it that way. And to her, treating me was a touchstone in her life." He was almost blushing. "Then there was this young Black doctor, he was the surgeon who operated on me. He had wanted to be a missionary doctor but became a surgeon instead and he sort of saw me as his patient and that he was doing his part to fight for civil rights by taking care of me."

"You got some emotional healing along with the physical healing," I thought aloud.

John nodded. "The other part of recovering from my anger is that amid that torture, I can remember like it was yesterday, it looked to me like there was a demonic shadow around those people who were beating me, like a shadow of devils—and that's when I recognized the unusual hatred those men had. I think it was there that I knew if I had an atomic bomb, I would release it there, and we would die there together. That's when I saw, and I guess this was God, that I was no better than them." I was shocked to hear him make that last statement. It seemed like a step too far to say he was no better than the racists who beat and tortured him.

"I don't see how I could have got to that level of hatred," John continued. "I saw I was no better than them and that's when I came to see the seed of reconciliation sown." His pace was quickening. "I think that's when I said 'Lord, if I get out of this jail tonight I want to preach a gospel that is strong enough to reconcile whites and Blacks to each other,' and boy when I got out of that jail, I didn't want to do that." It felt inappropriate but I laughed a bit at his admission.

"It was the pain after that that brought me to the conclusion that I would never be well unless I could forgive. And I have learned since then that's the only way you can deal with sin. There are not a lot of other ways. You've got to confess and you've got to ask God to forgive you and that's the only way, right?" He looked at me as if I could disagree.

"I have sin and it can be forgiven. It seems to me that this is what the Bible is talking about when the angel comes to Joseph and says "thou shalt call his name Jesus, for he shall save his people from their sin,"[1] and later Jesus says "If we confess our sins, he is faithful and just to forgive us our sins"[2] and "if we can't forgive those who sin against us, how do we expect our heavenly Father to forgive?"[3] There is no other way to deal with sin. I was finding out if my commitment to Christ was deep enough to see that I couldn't expect forgiveness from God if I didn't forgive these white men who beat and tortured me." He was tying his own forgiveness from God to the forgiveness he offered to the men who had beaten and tortured him as if it was the most logical conclusion.

I'm not in a position to disagree with John, but sometimes I'm tempted. He said he realized that he was "no better than them." "Them" being the men that beat him. Maybe he was speaking in hyperbole, but I suspect he wasn't. I suspect he believes it. He may be the most self-effacing man I've ever known. I wonder what it would be like to have the grace and mercy he does. I still don't know how he forgave them. It's difficult for me to think of them and forgive them, even though it didn't happen to me, and I wasn't even there.

The bigger part of this story is that John didn't just forgive white people in general and specifically the ones who had wronged him. John could have offered some kind of internal, mental forgiveness, but because he knew that the gospel is embodied and segregation was not the way of the kingdom, he went on to plant the Voice of Calvary congregation and community development organization, where interracial involvement was integral and considered foundational.

1. Matthew 1:21, KJV.
2. John 1:9, KJV.
3. Matthew 6:15, paraphrase.

What Is Forgiveness Really?

Sometimes people have trouble forgiving others because they have a fundamental misunderstanding of what forgiveness is. An all-too-common misconception is that forgiveness is to say that it's "okay" that an injustice took place. If this were the case then it would be just to withhold forgiveness because injustice is in fact *not* okay. In John's case, he knows well that the actions of those torturing him were not okay. No, forgiveness is releasing those who wronged us from owing us something for which they can't repay. Once an offense has occurred, it can't be undone. In a sense, there is nothing that can "make it right." If I snap at my children for something they've done, I can apologize immediately and take measures to make sure I handle the situation better next time, but still, the words are not unsaid. Thus we must forgive.

While forgiveness involves releasing control, that's not all there is to it. For us to move forward in emotionally healthy ways forgiveness entails wishing someone well. What I'm not saying is that forgiveness is letting a perpetrator off the hook. John sought justice against his perpetrators in the courts, and forgave them simultaneously. Forgiveness is a separate process from justice, and in fact many times to wish someone well probably means that they would face the consequences or discipline for their actions. After all, it's not good for us to hurt others and not see the damage done and learn from it, and sometimes that learning process involves some sort of restorative discipline.

At the end of the day, we can't control others. We can't make them sorry or contrite. We can't even always ensure that they face justice. What we do have control over is how much they and their actions control us in the aftermath. Forgiveness first and foremost releases us from the wrongs done to us.

Forgiveness isn't simply a spiritual concept detached from the real world. Loren Toussaint, a professor of psychology at Luther College, in 2015 helped edit *Forgiveness and Health*,[4] a book that detailed physical and psychological benefits. According to a story

4. Toussaint et al., eds., *Forgiveness and Health*.

on the website of the American Psychological Association "people who had greater levels of accumulated lifetime stress exhibited worse mental health outcomes. But among the subset of volunteers who scored high on measures of forgiveness, high lifetime stress didn't predict poor mental health. The power of forgiveness to erase that link was surprising. Toussaint says, 'We thought forgiveness would knock something off the relationship [between stress and psychological distress], but we didn't expect it to zero it out.'"[5]

It's funny how we so eagerly hang on to things that hurt us. It's like grabbing a hot burner on the stove and then stubbornly refusing to let go, as if we're punishing the stove by hanging on. Bitterness and resentment are the fruits of unforgiveness. Unchecked and unprocessed, they will rob us of peace within ourselves and with others.

This "abundant life"[6] that Jesus came to give isn't passively received, it's something that requires us to live into it. We can't sit back and nurture resentment and bitterness and expect that we'll just receive this abundant life that Jesus talked about. Jesus demands that we engage and participate in his life and everything that this entails, and there we will find abundant life.

Forgiveness Weaponized

On September 6, 2018, Amber Guyger, an off-duty police officer, entered the apartment of Botham Jean and murdered him as he sat in his living room eating ice cream and watching TV. Guyger said she believed the apartment was hers and Botham an intruder. The case gained national attention as another unarmed Black man had been killed by a police officer.

The resulting trial found Guyger guilty of murder. During the sentencing hearing Botham Jean's younger brother, Brandt, was given a chance to take the stand and address Guyger. Brandt's words appeared heartfelt and sincere. He encouraged Guyger to go

5. Weir, "Forgiveness can improve mental and physical health."

6. John 10:10.

to God for forgiveness, he told her he wanted the best for her, and the best would be for her to give her life to Christ. He forgave her and asked to give her a hug.

The scene was beautiful and incredibly moving. The video was shared and viewed over a million times. People, mostly white people, were quick to hold it up as a model of "what we need more of" and to use it to further certain ideologies beyond forgiveness. Others, mostly people of color, wisely saw that this act of forgiveness was being used to circumvent a conversation about justice.

If we're not careful we'll make forgiveness something that is owed to perpetrators (especially when we're the perpetrators), and we'll pervert reality by making oppressors out of the oppressed. Forgiveness is not something to be demanded from those we've wronged and it's not a tool used to escape the hard work of learning from our transgressions or their consequences. It's not to be used the muddy the waters of injustice. In this case, some were talking about the act of forgiveness as if forgiveness was primarily what America needs to quell racial strife and animosity, instead of the storied history and ongoing lie of white supremacy.

If you were a friend and I walked up to you and punched you in the face, you would probably become angry at me. What if I then became incredulous toward your anger and told you that the right thing for you to do is to forgive me? You might rightly point out that forgiveness is not the current issue, the current issue is that I don't seem to be taking responsibility for my actions; I don't seem to be sorry or contrite. What if I then quoted a Bible verse at you and told you that you just don't "get it"?

This is what is happening when white people say that what our country needs is forgiveness. It is misplaced and empty religiosity to demand forgiveness and not demand justice.

Wherever and Whoever You Are

This may seem all too big for you. The odds are that you've never been physically beaten because you were fighting for justice. We hear big stories of forgiveness on a grand scale like John's, or Black Africans toward the white minority in the aftermath of decades of apartheid, or a family forgiving someone who murdered their family member. My life is much more mundane than that, but truthfully we often struggle with forgiveness in the everyday mundanity of our lives.

Forgiveness is not just for professional peacemakers. It's for all of us—the stay-at-home dad, the woman working a nine-to-five, the pastor of the local church. If we don't forgive in the small things we can't forgive in the big things. We hold a grudge against those who have harsh words for us on social media. We rage when we're cut off in traffic. We have a family member who wronged us in the past and we've allowed bitterness and resentment to fester inside of us, or a friend that we haven't spoken to in years because of an argument we can't fully remember anymore. These small indiscretions are what make up a broken world as much as the large-scale violations and abuses. If we in our mundane lives can't learn the ways of forgiveness and mercy, then we'll surely never be able to access those qualities when life is most unfair. So how does John's story of forgiveness show us a way forward?

The Way of John and Jesus

One of the things John said really stood out to me. He said that when he was being beaten he felt like there was a demonic shadow over those men. It may not seem like much, but I think there is a really important lesson in forgiveness here. Paul in his letter to the church in Ephesus said: "For our struggle is not against enemies of blood and flesh, but against the rulers, against the authorities, against the cosmic powers of this present darkness, against the spiritual forces of evil in the heavenly places."[7]

A Christian view of conflict has to account for a spiritual realm at work. Although people have free will to do good or evil, they are not acting alone and John is right to attribute that level of

7. Ephesians 6:12.

hate to spiritual forces of evil. When we rightly see these spiritual forces behind the physical ones, we see perpetrators in the correct light and we're able to echo Jesus' words on the cross speaking about those crucifying him: "Father, forgive them; for they do not know what they are doing."[8]

In a Mood of Forgiveness

That day as we were finishing our conversation John told me, "You know, Shane, it's in a mood of forgiveness and love that I find myself in these days. I'm seeing this wonderful hope and I'm praying that God would use us, the church, to preach the gospel, a gospel that speaks to the evil of racism, and the evil of getting even. That's the kind of a feeling I'm feeling these days. That's what's driving me on."

If you want to see proof of God's love and power, look at John Perkins and his ability to forgive, to love in spite of a million reasons not to. I want to be like John.

Going Deeper

1. Is there someone you're withholding forgiveness from?

2. How is this holding you back from peacemaking?

3. Is there someone you need to ask for forgiveness?

4. How have you seen forgiveness weaponized?

Further Reading

The Very Good Gospel: How Everything Wrong Can Be Made Right, by Lisa Sharon Harper

8. Luke 23:34.

CHAPTER 5

Imagination and Creativity Is a Must

Boycotts Not Bullets

A MERICA HAS BEEN AT war for nineteen of the twenty years that I have been an adult. When in 2001 I saw the twin towers fall from the TV in my dorm room, I was about as war hungry as anyone else. We entered into a war in Afghanistan where we remained for about twenty years. Then not long after we went to war with Iraq. As the months turned into years, I and many others began to wonder if our military actions, trillions spent, and the lives lost made sense anymore. It seemed that alternatives to war should have at least been considered further.

Empires don't care much about being creative. Need more funds? Raise taxes. Need to protect an asset? Build a well-armed military. Need a foreign entity to cooperate with your agenda? Coerce through threats of sanctions or force. For peacemakers, however, the options of empires aren't available because by definition peacemaking doesn't happen by force or manipulative coercion.

Creativity is not just for artists, or at least for those that we normally call artists. I'm convinced that creativity fueled by a Christian imagination is a must-have skill in the tool belt of any Christ-follower who wants to be a peacemaker.

This talk of creativity in the context of peacemaking may seem strange. It may conjure images of painting nice murals on the side of a brick building in a big city—pictures of children of various skin tones holding hands together, with an inspirational tagline painted above. While I do think most public spaces *could* use more art, and there are times when traditional creative arts do play a role in peacemaking, this is not generally what we mean when we use the word *creativity* in this context.

Although John has not been in charge of geopolitical military conflicts, he has been a leader on the ground of the battle for civil rights, a battle in which using violence in lieu of creative measures seemed to some like a justifiable option. The creative ways that John and his friends figured out how to work within an unjust system opened my eyes to the possibilities in my own life when I'm tempted to go the easy way instead of the faithful way.

Attack or Avoid

Dan White, Jr., an author and church planting coach, describes a framework that can help us understand the role of creativity in peacemaking in his book *Love Over Fear: Facing Monsters, Befriending Enemies, and Healing Our Polarized World.*

"When something scares the daylights out of us, there are often two ways we deal with that scary thing: we attack it, or we avoid it. We are often pulled between these two responses," he writes.[1]

Attack or avoid. In war and in relationships often these are the only options we see. Someone at work has wronged us. We either attack by gossiping behind their back, sabotaging their efforts, or simply wishing ill upon them. Or maybe we avoid, by ensuring that we're not sitting next to them in the staff meeting, taking a route in the office where we're less likely to run into them, or by simply deciding they're someone you can't count on or collaborate with. Most of us only have an imagination for these two choices.

---

1. White, *Love Over Fear*, 69.

We live in a culture that enforces the idea that these are the only options available to us.

However, Christians have access to a God of creative possibilities, a God of third ways. John has embraced "third ways" throughout his life, especially when it would have been much easier to attack or avoid. In the aftermath of John's beating, he easily could have grown bitter towards white people. That may even have been the more reasonable thing to do. He could have decided that violence was a tool worth using. After all, it was a tool white folks hadn't hesitated to wield.

John also could have chosen to disengage with the civil rights movement, deciding that a government founded and dominated by white supremacy could never see change. He could have decided that the best thing he could do was to take care of himself and his, and accumulate as much wealth as possible to insulate himself and his family from the devastating effects of racism. He could have decided to be quiet—after all, his efforts had seemed to only put a target on his back. The world would have had to do without his books and nonprofits.

Engage

But John had creativity, and imagination, beyond attack and avoid. John's third way was to engage. I don't want to whitewash any of this. Engaging was not an easy choice. From our vantage point, seeing all of the success and attention that's come to John in the past fifty years, it might seem like engaging was the obvious and simple choice. What we have to keep in mind are the tremendous physical, emotional, and psychological toll that John's treatment at the hands of the white community took on him and his family. When we see a person of color extend forgiveness and engagement to white folks, that is often the tip of the iceberg. What we often don't see is the tremendous inner strength that brought them to that point—nights spent awake grieving the loss of security and safety they once felt in the world, and specifically for John, painful rehab from the physical damage to his body. To choose to engage over "attack" and "avoid" is not a default choice, it's a costly decision born of suffering, and one that may seem foolish in the moment.

The Boycott

I was at home. A fresh wave of violence between Israel and Palestine was in the news. It was hard to know where the news should register on my internal ranking of awful news. So far that year we had seen another spat of mass shootings. Walter Scott, an unarmed Black man, was killed by a police officer. Barely more than a week later Freddie Gray, a Black man, was arrested and put in a transport vehicle without being properly strapped in. During the transport he suffered spinal injuries that he would later die from. Earlier that month Dylan Roof, a white supremacist, walked into a Bible study at Emanuel African Methodist Episcopal Church in Charleston, South Carolina, and shot and killed nine people. Upon hearing the news of this most recent Middle Eastern conflict, it was as if I had failed to ration my feelings appropriately throughout the year and now I wasn't sure if my limited reserves could cover the grief I should have been having. As I had a few times before when I couldn't make sense of the world, I picked up the phone and called John. After our usual check-in, I blurted out: "Dr. Perkins, I know you did a lot of creative things when you were trying to get things to change in the civil rights era. Can you tell me them? Didn't you boycott something at some point?"

He didn't seem taken aback by my random question. "Well, my wife was the expert, of course, and I had to learn from others what she had organized. That happened the night we were locked in the jail in Mendenhall."

I was starting to remember more of the story. I had read about it some time ago. "Oh right, this was the time you had gone to bail someone else out?"

The details that I failed to remember in the moment were that a friend of John's had been arrested for drunken and disorderly conduct. Recently the sheriff's department had beaten up a member of John's church after arresting him on trumped-up charges. When John heard that this friend of his, also a Black man, had been arrested, he knew he needed to get him out of jail immediately. John showed up with his kids, some other kids from his church, and Doug Huemmer, a white civil rights worker. They knew the more people they took the less likely it was that the sheriff's deputies would try anything inappropriate.

"That jailer was just overpowered by our presence," John chuckled. "He didn't know what to do so he just locked us up in jail." The jailer sounded like a bit of a doofus.

"So Vera Mae decided to start this boycott to draw attention to your arrest?" I asked.

"Well, that night when we got locked up in jail, after some hours they let the kids out. They kept Doug and myself. They didn't beat us up. People came to the jail in mass to keep an eye on them so they couldn't do that. Everybody outside was worried they were 'beating up Doug and Grandpa JP.' The word was out, and that kept us from getting beaten. Because if we'd have gotten beaten up then it would have been a big deal. Black folks in town came to the jail outside, and because of the way the jail was built, I could speak to the people outside, from the jail."

John's friends outside were understandably angry. John even feared they might use violence to try to retaliate. From inside the jail he urged them not to give in and use the same means that white people had used against them. He knew they would lose everything if they gave into violence, including the moral high ground. John also told them something else. He told them that while they couldn't resort to violence, they also couldn't do nothing. John was refusing to pick the two options laid out for him, violence or nothing. John was choosing a third way. Those who gathered must have felt a sense of helplessness, but then John's refusal to give in to hate and violence allowed creativity to take over.

"That's when I got the idea for the boycott," John said. "The next morning on the street, Vera Mae and our friends were stopping all of the Black people who came into the town and telling them what had happened and not to buy anything in town until we were freed. This was just days before Christmas, and Black folks even had stuff on layaway they were going to pick up. After some time we did get out of jail, but they didn't stop the boycott. At some point, some civil rights lawyers came in and worked with us and said 'if you're going to boycott you've got to have some grievances, that the judge could agree to in court.' So, we wrote down a list of grievances and kept picketing!"

The boycott was effective in that Black folk banded together and in mass refused to buy things in Mendenhall stores. Soon white businesspeople and store owners were putting pressure on the police to let John and Doug go free. The boycott had sent a message. Now the Black folks of Mendenhall had a tool to resist the unfair practices they experienced. The boycott continued as long as Mendenhall didn't agree to amend that list of grievances. Their list included fair hiring practices, wages at least equal to the federal minimum wage, and fair treatment by law enforcement.

People with little power in society, those who are marginalized, often have a lot to teach the rest of us about creative imagination, and we would be wise to follow their leadership. Because marginalized people have little access to the kind of power that the privileged do, they're schooled in the use of creative imagination. John, Vera Mae, and those around them found a way to cause change and transformation that refused to resort to conventional corrupt or violent means.

Going Deeper

1. How could creativity play a role in a conflict you're currently experiencing?

2. Can you think of a time when the "attack" or "avoid" methods were used instead of "engage"? What was the outcome?

3. How do you think God has gifted you the creativity you need to face the antagonisms you face regularly?

Further Reading

- *Reconciling All Things: A Christian Vision for Justice, Peace and Healing*, by Emmanuel Katongole and Chris Rice
- *Love over Fear: Facing Monsters, Befriending Enemies, and Healing Our Polarized World*, by Dan White, Jr.
- *If Jesus Is Lord*, by Ron Sider

CHAPTER 6

Be Incarnational

The Three "R's"

H ERE IN AUSTIN, TEXAS where I live, there are people experiencing homelessness on almost every corner of our major
streets. From an early age our daughter had lots of questions about
the people standing on the medians at intersections holding up
cardboard signs. Once she understood that they didn't have homes
because they didn't have enough money, her next statement was,
"We should give them money so that they can get a home." I know
that was my first thought as a kid when I saw people experiencing
homelessness.

For most of us as we grow older and learn about the systemic
causes of poverty, we learn that there are often other factors at play,
that handing someone five dollars (or five *hundred*) alone can't
solve, like mental health issues, substance abuse, and systemic
inequalities. Many neighborhoods across the country suffer from
the effects of societal inequities.

I am not an expert on these issues, but the more I read and
talk to real experts, I realize that with all of the resources and
brilliant minds at work in relevant fields, there aren't many proven
strategies to help struggling communities. There are however,
many well-meaning white people and churches who inadvertently

do more harm than good. That's where I found myself before I learned about John's work.

I'm not a director of a nonprofit or a social worker. But I do live in a neighborhood of mostly people that don't look like me, and I want to give as much as I get. I first want to do no harm, and then I want to contribute. But like I said, there aren't many models out there to understand how to do that.

John Shares: The Three R's

The last time John and I had talked he told me he was about to be gone for awhile on an international trip.

A few weeks later we reconnected over the phone. "What was the trip for?" I asked him.

"I was at a conference for a global movement of people planting churches. Some of them are specifically using our three R's, which is becoming worldwide now. Of course some people were using the principles behind the three R's before we discovered them, but I think once we articulated them it gave people a biblical philosophy and it makes it easy for people to follow. So this group wanted me to come and sort of affirm that. More and more people are seeing the three R's as a virtue."

The Three R's

John developed what's now know as the three R's: relocation, reconciliation, and redistribution, out of the struggle he saw when he moved back to Mississippi in 1960.

Reconciliation

John's idea that reconciliation had to be a part of productive community development was born out of his pain in the aftermath of his beating by law enforcement. The reconciliation that John preaches is a reconciliation first between people and God, and then race to race and person to person. He insists on unifying the church's responsibilities to see to the spiritual and social needs of the world and refuses to divide them. He puts it in terms of "being" and "doing." We are "being" the church and that prompts us to action or "doing." We make the mistake of "being" without doing when we make the church into an enclave unto itself, being merely satisfied with our fellowship with each other. We make the mistake of "doing" without "being" when we think we can get on with our mission while leaving a pile of hurt and damaged people in our wake. Most churches that implode do so because they tried to "do" without "being" or "be" without "doing."

Since John and those around him started talking about reconciliation decades ago, the word has become frequently used in culture and sometimes overused to the point that there are cheap versions of reconciliation. Such cheap reconciliation requires nothing but tepid "let's just forget our differences and come together" sentiments. Real reconciliation, especially for those of us with power and privilege, involves confessing the wrong we've done both personally and systemically, asking for forgiveness, and repenting.

John envisions that our churches look like radically reconciled communities where "we are so secure in each other that we can share our feelings honestly without fearing rejection. We must create an environment where we confess our sins to each other, ask each other for forgiveness, and administer God's forgiveness to each other as his priests. And we must be able to lovingly confront one other and be willing to be confronted with our sins."[1]

Racial Justice

There has recently been some pushback against the term *reconciliation* when referring to racial reconciliation, preferring to instead use the term "racial justice." This is for good reason: after all, "reconciliation" is what happens when two parties come

1. Perkins, *With Justice for All*, 148.

back together. When in American history were Black and white people, as a group, *together*? Part of the ugly history and current reality of our story is that white people have failed to do what is necessary to be *together* with people of color. There have been of course beautiful exceptions and we would do well to study them and emulate them, but by and large, there are more examples of segregated churches and communities than there are diverse ones.

So how could we still in good conscience use the term *reconciliation*? For John, the reconciliation he preached was rooted in Christ and his church. So when he speaks of reconciliation, it's a cosmic concept. Because before all of this that we see today, before Jim Crow, before slavery, and even before the evil myth of racial difference was invented by those looking to profit from it, God created a good and beautiful world, and it was good. Humankind experienced union with God and each other. We know the rest of the story. Things went bad quickly, but the brokenness wasn't a part of how things were originally. Since then God has been on a rescue mission to bring back wholeness. Jesus came to earth as a part of that plan. Indeed an implication of the gospel is that God is inviting us to join him in this ongoing work of reconciliation.

Relocation

That day on the phone with John I was particularly interested in the second R of the three R's. Not that long ago, Kate and I scraped together all we could for a down payment and bought our first home, about a month after our first child was born. We were thrilled to be homeowners, but I knew with great privilege came great responsibility. The house was in a historically Black neighborhood, that was now predominately Latinx. I suspect the neighborhood had been underfunded and neglected by the city. When a hardware big-box store decided to move just a few miles further down the road to an up-and-coming planned community, they city bought the old building, used it for storage, and allowed the exterior to deteriorate and collect graffiti. Our new neighborhood was immediately behind the shell of this big-box store. So with all of this on my mind I was itching to ask John about how the relocation part of his three R's worked.

"Can I ask you specifically about relocation? It seems like the main idea is that you have to be in proximity to others to effect change. How did you figure out this was a key to being a peace-maker in a neighborhood?"

"Well, I told you before about how God opened the door for me to go into the public schools to teach the Bible. The state was building beautiful schools for Black folks for the first time because they thought that by doing that they could avoid the 1954 educational mandate from the Supreme Court to integrate. They were still trying to make 'separate but equal' work by appeasing Black folks with these nice schools. So for the first time, there were gyms, and much smaller class sizes. Because they were consolidating, they had more time not only to teach but for assemblies like the ones I would lead by telling a Bible story. There was no pressure in the South about the Bible in the public schools at that point. Inside the schools I saw that the education system was doing better at educating these children and was making some of these young people a success. The first Blacks to go to northern and western schools went mostly in the 1950s and 1960s because they began to need master's degrees and special degrees, and most had to go out of state to get a degree to teach in Mississippi."

"That couldn't have been good for those who stayed in Mississippi," I thought aloud.

"That's right," he said.

John went on to explain that there was a perfect storm brewing in Mississippi at that time. Many Black high school graduates were going off to college and never coming back. This made the existing Black population very old and very young, with not much in between. This exacerbated the lack of economic opportunity and quality of life for everyone who stayed. At the same time sharecropping was going away because farming was being mechanized. The outcome was that poverty in Mississippi was on the rise, and the state, in general, was getting poorer and poorer.

Seeing all of this happen in real time was one example of what led John to later create the three R's: Relocation, Reconciliation, and Redistribution.

John told me, "The three R's are just as relevant now as they were then, because many Black folks now integrate into white society and move out of their Black neighborhoods, and many white folks move out when they get too many Black folks in their neighborhoods."

John and Vera Mae's small church in Mississippi would reach four to seven high school students. "They would become a part of our church, but as soon as they graduated they were gone with no plan or desire to come back. And so I began to ask, 'How on earth are we going to improve the quality of life if the talent is going to leave?!' One night it hit me. I turned to Vera Mae and I said, 'Honey, I see what we've got to do. We've got to stay in this community long enough that we can win some of these young people to Christ, we've got to give them a love of God, a love of themselves, and a love of their communities, we've got to help them stay in school, tutor them, and help them to go off to college but also work with them to get them to come back to their communities.' So then was born that first 'R' of the three R's—'Relocation.' Relocating from the affluent places, *back* home to places of poverty. So as we began to talk about that, young whites from California and others were beginning to hear what we were doing, and they were coming down wanting to be a part of it."

The kind of relocation that John was interested in was mostly concerned with people indigenous to a town or neighborhood returning there after receiving education. I wanted to know what John thought about others relocating as well. "What do you think about outsiders with the right motivation relocated to under-funded neighborhoods as well? And how does someone relocate without bringing destructive gentrifying with them?" Truthfully, I wanted to know what he thought about *me* and my family moving to our new neighborhood.

"Yes, we had a fear of that," he replied. "And people in the neighborhood feared that the land was going to be taken up, driving up prices, and that the poor people were going to be overrun. We feared that when the new people came in, they were going to oppress the indigenous folks that were already there. We were afraid that those indigenous folks were going to have to move out."

"We asked ourselves some questions," he told me.

"How can we harness the change in a neighborhood?"

"How can we bring that poor minority into prosperity?"

"How do we plant churches there?"

"How do we plant community there, or stabilize those communities in a way that we harness the energy and enthusiasm of the new transplants?"

John said the writing of a guy named Bob Lupton really helped them do this well. Bob came out of the Christian Community Development Association (CCDA), the organization that John helped pioneer that went on to implement the three R's in neighborhoods. Bob's idea was to go into neighborhoods and help the people indigenous to that neighborhood to empower them to have ownership of the neighborhood and stabilize the community. So the CCDA went into neighborhoods and began to buy old apartments. They began to stabilize, remodel, and keep the people in the community. In short they made it possible for the poor to rise along *with* a changing community. Through organizations like the CCDA bigger pools of money were allocated to buy major pieces of land and major buildings. Suddenly apartments could be turned into condos because, as John says, "owning real estate is an investment that people can take part in, whereas when you're paying rent you never see that money again."

When people have access to loans, where organizations help educate people on homeownership and money management, people and communities are in a much better situation.

"It's all about harnessing what's already there in a community, harnessing the indigenous people," John said. "They'd buy into the neighborhood, and keep their place in it, whether that be in a downtown area or anyplace else. That way, they *also* benefit from the changing of the community, by way of new jobs closer to where they live. Of course, unless we act, very often the residents will be forced out. When that happens, people are often driven to the sub-urbs, and the poverty in the suburbs is rising fast. That's no good because the services that many in poverty would find helpful aren't located in the suburbs. Think about bus routes, food pantries, and nearby businesses."

I knew that poverty was growing fastest in the suburbs but I never considered the implications. So many public services are concentrated in urban centers.

John continued, "So I think a combination of all affordable housing and homeownership among people indigenous to the neighborhood slows up gentrification and hopefully enriches the community."

Of course the three R's are flexible and that's important be-cause often for incarnational ministry, contextualization is key.

When John lived in Pasadena, California, he encouraged rei-magining existing spaces. Where a big mansion existed, it could be torn down and multiple dwellings built in its place. Then, John's organizations could bring in many families and subsidize twenty of the units. The rest of the area might become gentrified, but now there are more low-income people there than there would be oth-erwise. A block that housed just a few people before might have 150 people now. The key is to work on the neighborhood level, with people indigenous *to* the neighborhood, invest in urban ar-eas, and help those in poverty.

Going To vs. Being With

Before my family and I lived in Austin we lived in a small town in central Texas. There was a small neighborhood that consisted of a few streets of houses, and a block of government housing. Being in the middle of Texas, a very "churched" area and culture, there were tons of churches in the town, as well as a small Christian universi-ty. The churches and the university had various programs directed at the people who lived in government housing. Sometimes they would help with physical needs like food, school supplies, or a ride to the store. Some would lead after-school programs or summer Bible clubs for the kids. Some would simply visit with the people who lived there. In all of my years of living in that town and being connected with various churches and ministries, I never knew or even heard of anyone moving into the neighborhood. For most people, you got to the government housing block by getting in a church van. It wasn't a place to live.

I don't tell that story to point a finger at "those selfish church people." Notice that I myself lived in the town for years but never moved into the neighborhood either. No doubt those church folks did a lot of good and were real friends to some of the people living on that block. What I can say is that I also never heard of anyone escaping the conditions that required them to live in government housing, aside from some very hardworking and incredibly intelligent children that spent some time growing up there. For the most part, the Christians in town played the role of a firefighter, putting out fires in people's lives or addressing momentary needs and shortages. That's no small thing, but I would hesitate to call it transformation.

Neighborhood Champions

Living in a low-income neighborhood isn't for everyone. But for those who don't they should at least be asking how they can encourage and support those who do, especially those who are indigenous to the neighborhood and either never left or came home after leaving.

Often those who are from a neighborhood are those best at bringing transformation to that neighborhood. In his book *Red, Brown, Yellow, Black, White—Who's More Precious In God's Sight?*,[2] pastor and nonprofit director Leroy Barber calls these people "neighborhood champions."[3] According to Barber,

---

2. Barber, *Red, Brown, Yellow, Black, White.*
3. Barber, *Red, Brown, Yellow, Black, White*, 50–51, 53–54, 59, 62.

> Almost all neighborhoods already have champions, people who have lived there a long time, or were born there and returned, and perhaps are second or third generation. They represent God and do good among their neighbors. They may not have much in terms of resources (often because of their sacrificial giving or concentration on service rather than generating income), yet they find ways to help, support, and empower people despite their economic condition. Much of their work goes unnoticed or overlooked.[4]

For outsiders moving into a neighborhood, supporting neighborhood champions is a must, and it's one element that delineates the "relocation" that John talks about from destructive gentrification. As Barber says, neighborhood champions may not have much in terms of resources, but imagine the transformation that could take place from the synergy of new neighborhood transplants getting behind and following the lead of a neighborhood champion, by contributing some of those resources, be they financial, educational, or otherwise.

I want to give a word of warning here. Neighborhood transplants can unwittingly do damage to a community by going in with the wrong attitude and expectations. Paternalism and a savior complex have wreaked havoc in the lives of transplants and those indigenous to the neighborhood. Transformation is not fast and it's not easy, and no one is waiting for middle-class white people to save the day.

The Legacy of John's Relocation

It's difficult to overemphasize the impact of the three R's. If you've studied poverty, you know that it is a complex problem and many brilliant minds have tried and failed to make a real difference. The Christian Community Development Association, which John pioneered, took his original three R's and expanded them into eight key components, by adding: leadership development,

4. Barber, *Red, Brown, Yellow, Black, White*, 47.

empowerment, wholistic approach, church-based, and listening to the community. The eight key components aren't magic bullets, but they have transformed communities and changed lives. All of this happened because John and his family refused to simply be outsiders or interlopers. They lived with and amongst the people he was called to help.

Relocating for All of Us

In my work in real estate, I regularly see Christians who are looking for a house motivated almost exclusively by "good schools" and "safe neighborhoods." While I sympathize and it's natural to want those things, I'm disheartened that there aren't more Christians who don't hear a call to live amongst people of different socio-economic and ethnic backgrounds. I don't think most of us white people realize that the schooling choices we make, be they home-school, charter school, or public school, may have harmful effects on children of color in poorer schools.

I'm praying that more white Christians wake up to these realities of how their seemingly innocuous lifestyle choices are counterproductive to transformation and a Christlike life. Too many of us don't even have an imagination for moving outside our front door. One of the things John has helped me see is how relocation is accessible for every Christian willing to step outside of their own world.

Some friends of mine, a white, middle-class married couple and their kids, live across the street from a Latinx family. My friends had a few conversations with them coming and going, but struggled to make a deeper connection.

In a homogenous neighborhood, these connections are easier. Coming from the same socioeconomic and ethnic background gives you shared experiences and often shared lenses with which to view the world. If I meet another white guy around my age I probably don't have to try for very long to find a common interest—Indie-folk music, Wes Anderson movies, eighties movies in general. It can be more difficult for nonhomogeneous groups to form a bond. Faced with this difficulty, my friend decided just to be present and available when possible.

Eventually, my friends got frustrated that they hadn't made more of a connection with the family across the street. They decided to ask them over for dinner. They thought, "We all eat, right?" The evening came and the family of five showed up at their door. The parents speak little English and my friends speak little Spanish. There were some awkward silences and misunderstandings in the conversation as there often are when language barriers exist. The two younger boys were very quiet and soon after eating said something about homework and dismissed themselves to go back to their home across the street. The couple's teenage daughter was mostly quiet when my friend asked her about her school and extracurricular activities. Then he asked her about movies and TV shows and her eyes lit up. She and my friend talked in detail about her favorite shows and those they'd both seen.

My friends asked the couple where they met, which led to a conversation about their home country of Mexico and their time in the US. Without much lead-up, the husband began talking about the trouble the Trump administration had been causing for their family and friends. A relative of theirs had recently been rounded up in an ICE raid. They themselves aren't citizens but didn't seem to be worried about a threat of deportation. My friends listened to their story and conveyed their sympathy. Before this interaction, they cared deeply about the plight of immigrants in a political environment that was hostile towards them, but until then the issue had been just that, an issue. They didn't know anyone personally that had been affected, it was just something they lamented and shook their heads at when they listened to the news. Now it was different, more personal.

That night when their neighbors were leaving the gratitude they expressed was some of the most sincere and earnest that my friend had ever seen. They were truly happy to be spending time with my friend and his family. Sometime later, the family invited my friends to their house for dinner. The friendship is growing.

That story is small. It's only a start. But I'm convinced that these small starts reverberate in our communities and hearts. My friend Jeremy Courtney founded an amazing organization in Iraq called Preemptive Love Coalition. In its time PLC has provided heart surgeries for Iraqi children and provided on the ground life-sustaining supplies for refugees and internally displaced people escaping violence. I remember clearly one night when Jeremy shared about the latest work of PLC. The danger level of Jeremy and his family's work in Iraq had vacillated during their time there. At that particular time, tensions between some Muslims and Westerners were particularly high because of some recent terrorist attacks that some Westerners had unfairly seen as the fault of all Muslims and Middle Easterners. Jeremy told us that the best thing we could do to contribute to the safety of Westerners working in NGOs in the Middle East was to go meet a Muslim in our town. Jeremy wasn't suggesting making a project out of anyone; he simply knew the power of friendship. As Brené Brown says, "People are hard to hate close-up."[5]

That is the power of relocation. It can change things on the other side of the world. This is true if the relocation is across the world, across town, or across the street. This isn't some new idea rooted in progressive ideals of social justice. This is rooted in the gospel itself. As John reminded me, "It was God who first relocated and came to live amongst us."

Redistribution

In the last several years the population of the United States has become more polarized, partisan, and hyper-political. This atmosphere makes it difficult to use a word like *redistribution*. Say that word a lot and you'll have someone accuse you of being a socialist. While I think it's good for us to rethink the sacred place that capitalism occupies in our hearts, especially the kind of hyper-consumeristic capitalism we see in place today, the kind of

---

5. Brown, *Braving the Wilderness*, 63–83.

redistribution John referred to in the 3 R's isn't about socialism. It is simply about Christians individually and corporately being purposeful about what they do with their time, money, and resources, and using those assets to help the people Jesus called us to care about.

Redistribution is closely linked to the previous "R," relocation, because often relocation causes redistribution and redistribution happens more frequently, easily, and naturally when relocation has taken place. When someone with educational and financial resources moves into an underserved neighborhood they bring those resources with them. If their child goes to the neighborhood public school and they volunteer to help out in the classroom or PTA just as they would if they were in a middle- or upper-class neighborhood, now they are redistributing their time, education, and finances to that underserved neighborhood. When they hire neighbors for services they would normally find off the internet, they are spending their money on people who could benefit most from it instead of large corporations that disproportionately benefit those at the top of the ladder.

In talking about redistribution, John recalled a project that his organization, the John and Vera Mae Perkins Foundation, has undertaken. It is called the Zechariah 8 Housing Program, or Z8 for short. Z8 provides housing for single parents and others who would otherwise be unable to afford it.

A few years ago I visited John in Jackson. He drove me around the neighborhood where Z8 is located, pointing out all of the houses the foundation had purchased for Z8. While the homes were older, they had been improved and made into good homes. As we passed each house John told me what the foundation had paid for each house. My jaw dropped. Real estate in Jackson was *much* cheaper than in Austin, where I live. What a wonderful opportunity for Christians to invest in housing for those who need it.

Habitat For Humanity is a well-known organization that helps redistribute resources to those who need it. John mentioned to me that HFH was one of the organizations that he saw early on and modeled many of his principles of community development.

There's an organization here in Austin called Mobile Loaves & Fishes. As their website says, "More than two decades ago, Mobile Loaves & Fishes' founders boldly answered God's call to 'love your neighbor as yourself.'"[6] In its early days, MLF simply delivered food and provisions to those living on the streets. Today MLF has a fifty-one-acre master-planned development that includes tiny homes to house those formerly experiencing homelessness, enterprises to provide work that include a community inn, a cinema, a garden, a car wash, an inspection station, and more.

So we can see that far from a pipe dream or socialist contexts, the idea of redistribution is alive and thriving in organizations all over the country and world.

The Call of Christ

Christians would do well to wake up to the reality that the call of Christ is embodied, and the three R's are a beautiful embodiment of that call. Although this embodiment of Christ in our lives will look somewhat different for each of us, all Christians should in prayer ask God to open their eyes to show them where he is at work, and then join in that work. If we genuinely and consistently pray this prayer then we will be surprised at the opportunities that present themselves and how the opportunities will most likely involve relocation, reconciliation, and redistribution.

Going Deeper

1. Are the three R's a new concept to you? Are there ways that you've seen relocation, reconciliation, and/or redistribution happen with beneficial results?

2. How do you think God might be prompting you to participate in relocation, reconciliation, and/or redistribution?

---

6. Mobile Loaves & Fishes, "About Us."

3. Think of one person or family that is in close proximity to you, and invite them over to your house for a meal. It could be a neighbor, or maybe a coworker. Be sure to listen more than you talk.

Further Reading

- *Beyond Charity: The Call to Christian Community Development*, by John Perkins
- *Red, Brown, Yellow, Black, White—Who's More Precious In God's Sight?: A Call for Diversity in Christian Missions and Ministry*, by Leroy Barber
- *The Power of Proximity: Moving Beyond Awareness to Action*, by Michelle Ferrigno Warren

CHAPTER 7

Pursue Diversity

John's Multiracial Community in the South

T HE DAY WAS SUNNY and I had called John with no particular agenda other than to catch up. He was just back from a trip at a conference in Malaysia. I asked all the usual travel questions about his flight and how the food was. Since the conference was about churches and I knew nothing about the church in Malaysia, I asked him about that.

John Shares:
A Homogenous Church or an Obedient Church

"I saw churches trying to bring peace, and Christians trying to reveal an authentic gospel."

"Really?!" I wasn't expecting such a potent answer.

"Shane, the great implication of the gospel is that it's holistic. The gospel illuminates relocation, reconciliation, and redistribution. It represents the fullness of life. We've come to call it 'holistic Christian community development,' concern for the body, concern for the soul, and concern for all the aspects of people's lives."

"Say more about that holistic gospel," I prodded.

"For the last twenty-five years we've been trying to 'fill the holes in,' the things we've missed, those holes that accommodated injustice, racism, bigotry. The church has not dealt with them. The church ended up being segregated and homogenous. For the most part, Christians accepted it and planted churches *based* on homogeneity. I think, now, we are realizing the damage that's been done, and planting these new intentionally diverse churches is the best way to deal with it. There are other issues that the church has to deal with, but homogeneity in the church is so insidious. It's counter to the gospel. The idea of racism is that it's always going to be here. But for the church to accept it is a contradiction to the gospel. You understand?"

I did, and I was excited to talk about it because I had been looking for direction. "Yes! Yes, completely. I'm glad we're talking about this. A diverse church is something that I realize I personally need to experience, really we all do, but as I'm looking out there, there aren't tons of churches that are really diverse."

Generally, a church is considered to be diverse when it has no more than 80 percent of one racial group. Baylor University found that while one in four Catholic churches are diverse, only 12 percent of Protestant churches are considered diverse.[1]

So, I asked John, "Why do we still seem to be segregated?"

"Yes, the reasons are many. Boy, we could talk for a long time about that, all of the reasons. It's cultural. It's historical. It's expedient. It's easier in many ways to be homogenous, but the easy way is almost never the best way. If we're honest about it, we should consider that a disobedient sin. Sin is our selfish desire. We don't see homogeneity as one of our selfish desires, but it is. We don't see that as disobedience, but it is. We see it as normal, you know? We don't hear that in the gospel, even though it's there. We don't hear and consider the words of Scripture: "And whosoever will, let him take the water of life freely."[2] It doesn't occur to us that we're disobeying God or sinning, but we're wrong. It is sin."

---

1. Dougherty and Emerson, "The Changing Complexion."
2. Revelation 22:17b.

I wasn't sure I was following his logic, but I've learned that with John, if you can hang on and keep up you'll understand in the end.

"A commission is an instruction and or a command. So the Great Commission[3] is an instruction and command, by God, for us to go into *all* the world and preach the gospel to every ethnic group."

I was starting to see where this was going.

"If we believe we can do that without forming multicultural churches," John continued, "we're kidding ourselves. Most churches and pastors have the opinion that because they don't actively discriminate it's not a problem that they're homogenous. They would say, 'I'm preaching the gospel to everybody. They didn't come and join our church. It's their fault.'"

I had heard this exact thing before. Honestly, it probably wasn't that many years back that I had thought the exact same thing.

"Yes, that's exactly right! That opinion is probably the most prevalent," I said.

"Yes. 'It was open, but they didn't come.' People say that to me all the time. Well, we need to look and see what's within us, what we're *not* preaching. Are we preaching the type of gospel that has God's Holy Spirit within itself? Are we preaching the sword of the spirit, which is the word of God? Is that word of God 'quick and powerful,'[4] delivered 'sharper than any two-edged sword,'[5] that pierces to the 'asunder of soul and spirit . . . joints and marrow, and is a discerner of the thoughts and intents of the heart'?[6] Is that the gospel we're preaching? We should ask that question, but we're not asking that question."

He was getting fired up. I like it when John gets fired up.

---

3. Matthew 28:16–20; Mark 16:14–18; Luke 24:44–49; Acts 1:4–8; John 20:19–23.

4. Hebrews 4:12.

5. Hebrews 4:12.

6. Hebrews 4:12.

"We act like the Spirit is just picking out those it desires to join us and we aren't called to partner with God. We have more than that in the Great Commission.[7] We have an intention. It's simple, are we obeying God or disobeying God, you know? We have become so accustomed to racism, in that we have accepted that our churches won't break through that barrier, and we have accepted a gospel that is less than multicultural."

More Than Just Leaving the Door Open

It's true, most white churches don't actively and intentionally discriminate, most would even like to be more diverse, but few are willing to do the work and lay down the power that would be required to break up homogeneity.

For starters, many white churches haven't taught any theology around race. They don't know much about the myth of racial difference and don't have a vision for the people of God being a people group of their own[8] that recognizes and actively rejects anything that dehumanizes people, and that white supremacy is a dehumanizing system that pervades our culture. In this environment, a church could do more damage to people of color by having them in their doors but perpetuating evil patterns that people of color experience regularly in the culture at large. Only now the patterns have the veneer of Jesus on top of them. That idea should leave us in disgust and prompt us to lament and repent.

White Christians would do well to attend a Black or other predominantly non-white church, simply observe, and ask ourselves some questions. What's the first thing I experience when I walk in? What do I hear and see around me? How is the space decorated? What is the music like? How would you describe the preaching style? What is the congregation's reaction to what

---

7. Matthew 28:16–20; Mark 16:14–18; Luke 24:44–49; Acts 1:4–8; John 20:19–23.

8. This is the same as being "colorblind" and doesn't mean that we stop recognizing the gifts that come from our ethnicities. Quite the opposite.

is going on? Do the children stay during the service? How does everyone else receive you?

My guess is that this exercise would be eye-opening, and would start to help us see the differences between the way white people tend to do church and why our spaces may not be as inviting as we once thought. The goal isn't to simply expropriate or appropriate a certain aesthetic into white churches, but to fundamentally rethink and rebuild our churches based on something other than what seems right to white people, something that acknowledges the power in the voices of people of color.

John Shares: Taking Action

I wanted to know what John had to say about all of this. "So how do churches become more diverse once they realize homogeneity is a problem?"

"It won't happen naturally. Some churches in the suburbs have say 2 to 5 percent integration of people not from the majority culture in that community. That 2 to 5 percent who want a church nearby will find these churches and will go there naturally. They will enjoy that, but that generally would only be middle-class people. But we want to reach *all* people. We want to especially try to reach our folks who are in bad social conditions and amid economic deterioration. So in planting multiracial churches, we're better equipped to give attention to the broken people in our society. Now, on the practical side, I think churches can become more diverse just by talking about it."

"By just acknowledging out loud that being diverse is something that they want to do?" I asked.

"That's one thing. Also, churches have to think outside of their traditional mind-set. For instance, there are some small towns where colleges are more diverse than the population of the town, so I think that we should be reaching out to the colleges in town. Reaching young people in general is helpful because there are a growing numbers of young people who see racial diversity as a virtue. Next, it's important to teach people that there's joy in diversity and removing malice in our hearts. We should be intentional about giving testimony of the richness of our fellowship, and show everyone that our fellowship is richer because we are intentionally obeying God." I could hear joy in his voice at the thought of such a fellowship.

"What about making sure that churches have people of color on staff and in leadership positions?" I asked. This was something I had heard from other church leaders championing diversity. It seems that giving or sharing power is an important step in becoming diverse, instead of just *hoping* that people of color just show up to white churches.

"Yes!" John said. "I think there has to be a strategic plan. That's part of what I mean when I use the phrase 'intentional churches.' The churches that Paul oversaw assumed that there were 'neither Jew nor Gentile, foreign nor free, male or female, but we were one in Jesus Christ.'[9] Somewhere along the line, we, the church, sold out, or better yet, accommodated to the cultural racism and the cultural classism. It was never intended by Christ because he created us in his image. That's what we have to reclaim. We are not quite there yet. We are not quite there, and honestly, we are not quite ready to see racism as evil. It's difficult. We practiced it for so long, I think we have not been able to repent sufficiently."

It may seem overly pessimistic or even harsh to hear John say we're not ready to see racism as evil. After all, could you imagine any Christian leader claiming that racism is anything but evil? But the sad truth is that if the Christian church truly believed that racism was evil our churches would be more diverse and white Christians would be accomplices with their brothers and sisters of color in the struggle for societal equality.

When John said that we have not been able to repent sufficiently, he was touching on something important, the role of lament in dealing with our past. Professor and author Soong-Chan Rah rightly points out that the American church's need to lament its part in the darkest of America's history.

---

9. Galatians 3:28.

A contemporary funeral dirge for the twenty-first-century American church would require the effort to more fully understand and learn another's history. It could be as simple as watching films that depict the atrocities of the slave trade and the institution of slavery. It may involve visiting museums that teach the history of racism in the United States. It may require a deepening understanding by reading texts that engage this often hidden history. The knowledge of this history can begin the process toward an authentic lament. The church must engage in a funeral dirge that reflects the truth of our tainted history.[10]

John echoed Rah's sentiments. "We're bound with racism because we have not repented and been able to see it as being sinful. We might see it as a mistake. The sentiment you hear is that it's something that people ought not to have done, having slaves, 'but that is such a long time ago. They ought to be over it by now.' 'I didn't participate in that,' they say."

John is leading us to something important here: We're missing the point if we think our action steps are to simply gear our outreach efforts to a more diverse population (although most churches would do well to think about that). Instead, white churches must walk each other through the hard work of educating ourselves on how racism has taken hold in our culture and in our hearts, and then dismantle it.

John as usual had spent a lot of time with me. I felt like I needed to let him get back to his day. But I couldn't resist asking one more thing. "So with all of that in mind, how do you think a church leader could explain to a church, or maybe even just someone to their friends, the concepts of white privilege, and the lasting effects of systemic oppression?"

He collected his thoughts. "I think that would have to be a part of the overall teachings, and the greatest tool for helping people see these truths, of course, is telling them about God's deep love, the incarnation and his shedding his blood. He loves us so much that He forgives us and then invites us to join his redemption

10. Rah, *Prophetic Lament*, 51–52.

work. We model out that deep love for each other. I think that's the kind of living, as well as the teaching, we need to go about. I think, as a part of that, we need to remind people of that, praying that the Holy Spirit will open their eyes. More and more, now, I'm trying to think about new birth, trying to encourage people to seek that supernatural expression of God's love in our lives, and that supernatural forgiveness, so that we can actually be reconciled, and then plan our lives together."

I was floored. It seems, the way John sees it, what people need to know about white privilege and other more difficult nuances involved in issues of race were all encompassed in the single message of God's deep love for us, or as John put it to me later, "our friendship with God." I realized something in that moment: It's not that John believes that we shouldn't teach explicitly about these concepts. On the contrary, it's precisely because these concepts are encompassed in God's love for us that we should teach about them. Once we know and feel God's great love for us, and really receive it, our need to be on top fades away.

Going Deeper

1. The last time you looked for a church to be a part of, was racial diversity included in your desired criteria? Why or why not?

2. What do you think your church could do to be more diverse?

3. What preferences are you willing to give up in order for your church to be a more diverse community?

Further Reading

- *Disunity in Christ: Uncovering the Hidden Forces that Keep Us Apart*, by Christena Cleveland

CHAPTER 8

We Have to Know Our History

John Remembers Schools, Housing, and Healthcare

IN A NOW-FAMOUS TED Talk,[1] lawyer and social justice activist Bryan Stevenson told a story of a talk he once gave in Germany about criminal justice and specifically the death penalty. Afterward, someone approached him and said "We can never have the death penalty in Germany. . . . There is no way, with our history, we could engage in the systematic execution of human beings. It would be unconscionable." Stevenson went on to call attention to the long history of systemic oppression of Black people in America that started with the slave trade, followed by Jim Crow. He then went on to imagine if Germany not only had the death penalty but if it was disproportionately killing Jewish people. Germany realizes that their history matters and it informs the way it acts as a society. Contrast this with America's own track record of brutality against Black people. Still our criminal justice system incarcerates and executes Black folks disproportionately.

One thing I learned from John through his books, even before we met, is that history matters and we have to choose to learn from our history and let it inform our future. Those who are

1. Stevenson, "We need to talk about an injustice."

serious about peacemaking must be aware of history, the history of our country, states, cities, and even the neighborhoods, if we want to bring healing instead of more hurting.

John Shares: History Speaks

I had John on speakerphone. Recently I was rereading through one of John's old books, *A Quiet Revolution*, and I had few questions. "Dr. Perkins, I wanted to ask you about the conditions that African Americans have lived through in the past that contribute to their plight today. In *A Quiet Revolution*, you quoted James Silver: 'Silver said that for a black in Mississippi, everything in his environment was designed to make him feel inferior . . . Once he accepted that, then he could appear to be happy. The white man could say then, "See, our blacks are very happy with the life they're living."'[2]

What's striking to me about that is that so many people think the same today. People think Black folks are treated fairly in society and have the same amount of opportunity as white people.

John said, "Well, Senator Daniel Moynihan predicted what was going to happen with the path that we were on, in 'The Moynihan Report.'"[3]

John told me that "The Moynihan Report" was officially called "The Negro Family: The Case For National Action." In 1965, when the "Report" was written, people were optimistic that the civil rights act and other civil rights legislation would change the plight of poor Black people. But Moynihan knew that it would take more than that, and grew frustrated that people in government weren't seeing that. Moynihan stated that the Black community had endured "three centuries of sometimes unimaginable mistreatment," and that the Johnson administration and society in general had underestimated the damage done by those three centuries. So Moynihan wasn't just saying that Jim Crow had ramifications, but that 300 years of oppression had ramifications.

2. Perkins, *A Quiet Revolution*, 17
3. Moynihan, "The Negro Family."

I observed, "It sounds like someone might read 'The Moynihan Report' and they could say, 'Okay, inequality today is caused by racism of the past,' but we *still* have conditions today, like Silver mentioned, that are there to make Black folks 'feel inferior.'"

John responded, "Right, we *still* have ghettoes and not only have the white folk moved out but there are forces that have trapped many Blacks there. History is key to understanding how we got where we are. For instance, the history of how social programs developed and changed. Take Aid to Families with Dependent Children, for example. That was aimed at children who lived in low-income families. As white women beginning in the 1940s and 1950s started joining the workforce, those families now could bring in Blacks who were migrating in and pay them cheaply to be their maids and household employees. Then when these Black women became pregnant and had to take time off, white women, instead of paying them during that time off, would help their maids to get on welfare while these babies were being born. So these white families were benefiting from this system of welfare and many of these Black mothers, as they had more babies, could make more money having these babies and putting them on welfare than they could with the job they had. Now, who do you blame for that? It was welfare for those white families. To look back and blame Black people for getting on welfare is to fault the victim and not those who benefited from the welfare. This was part of a larger system. Of course, there were almost no Black legislators to call the system into question."

That's the first time I had ever heard this. "Wow," I said. "To make sure I'm hearing you right, a white family would hire a Black woman to do their domestic work and then they would 'help' them get on welfare so that they didn't have to either pay them enough so that they could survive while they took time off for any kind of maternity leave, or pay them through maternity leave? The government was effectively subsidizing the lifestyles of white families through welfare?"

"Right," said John, "and especially when they liked these ladies, because they were taking care of their children, and sometimes the nanny would have three children of her own. She can't come to work, but there's a welfare system that she would have told them about and probably would have still had her come some days, even being on welfare. This is anecdotal but this is the kind of thing I saw in the South. And of course social security for Black folks didn't really come until the fifties for rural Mississippians."

"Wait, social security didn't come for Black folks until the fifties?!" I couldn't believe what I was hearing and I couldn't believe I had never heard it before.

John explained, "When the Social Security Act was passed in 1935 it excluded farmworkers and maids, which was two-thirds of working Blacks in the South. That didn't change until the 1950s. Many of those people were probably being paid cash under the table too, I would assume. Back then ain't nobody going to question it, ain't no government going to question that."

I had to make sure I was keeping up. "Oh. You mean it was the way of life to have that cheap labor and not even the US government, including the IRS, run almost exclusively by white people, wanted to disrupt that way of life."

"Right!," said John. "Are you going to disrupt all of the white ladies? You have to keep in mind, the white ladies didn't have participation in the government until the turn of the century, and most of the congressmen were white men, and these were their wives. So you've got an unjust system there that you're going to upset if you start asking questions."

John went on to say that there were many of those kinds of official means of oppression at that time. In Mississippi the Sovereignty Commission, under the guise of being a respectable citizens group, while harboring the ethos of the KKK, enjoyed the support of the state, and used it to subjugate Black folks. And the church accommodated it. These were white church people that were doing this, and Black people, mostly Black *church* people, were suffering because of it. Those that rebelled against the system were locked in jail or killed.

Of course police couldn't put someone in jail for fighting racism. They had to name a crime committed. For many during the civil rights era the crime they were accused of committing was "disturbing the peace" or "indecent exposure." In the civil rights marches people would often get arrested for peeing in the streets. If you went back and looked at arrest records of Black folks in marches, you might see that many of the arrests were for 'indecent exposure,' because there weren't bathrooms available during the marches, and they couldn't have gone into a white bathroom if it was available.

Hearing all of this from John was compelling. "I hear you, Dr. Perkins, but I can imagine some white folks hearing this and then saying, 'Yeah, that's the way it worked back in the 1960s, but why do Black families still struggle today?'"

John said, "There are a lot of complex reasons for that, that many people have spent years studying, so we need to be careful not to be too simplistic about it. But what we can say is that an entire system contributed to making the lives of Black people harder. Look at what's happening in some of our major cities: they're being rebuilt and Black folks had been cramped in the ghettoes, but now those neighborhoods are being torn down and gentrified. Now these Black folks are forced out to the suburbs, where it's more difficult to have access to work by the bus and commuter system. As a result, many of the middle-class people in suburbia are gating their communities or semi-gating them. I'm not totally against gating because we do need some form of community and we need some boundaries. It's not all a conspiracy, but it is a bigger system, an evil one. Paul would say it in terms of wrestling 'not against flesh and blood but against principalities.'"[4]

John continued, "We tend to organize power for our own advantage. Look at how powerful companies outsource work to Bangladesh or China or Haiti or to other places in the world where you can get the labor so much cheaper. And if companies do keep work in the US, they pay as little as possible. Now in the US, we see that the minimum wage isn't enough to support families. I would suspect that folks who live in gated communities, in general, are more against a livable wage."

4. Ephesians 6:12.

I've seen what John was talking about firsthand. I'm with John in not being opposed to gated communities as an absolute, but I have seen segregation keep us away from witnessing the consequences of the policies we support and vote for. It's not so much that we middle- and upper-class people who think this way are heartless and uncaring, it's that our lifestyle prevents us from having to see and think about the real-world effects of those positions. And so the system goes on.

John Speaks: Education

"Dr. Perkins, my family lives in this diverse neighborhood, but doesn't want to be part of the negative effects of gentrifying. When it comes time to send our kids to school, how can we help instead of harm?"

John answered, "Most of the people who are moving back to those once-neglected neighborhoods are not moving back to hurt people intentionally, but harmful gentrification naturally will take place if the new residents aren't intentional. You would have benefitted because you could buy an affordable house, and have a good quality of life, but most importantly you would also be there trying to love your neighbor as you love yourself and that will bless people in ways you don't think about."

"Your kids are going to be there in the same schools with other kids, some of whom statistically might be at risk for dropping out, and you're going to be giving your kids educational support at home that your college education enabled you to give. Your kids are in turn going to be participating alongside their classmates, and if they're doing that, they themselves are still going to get a good education, and helping others to learn will give them a sense of fulfillment. Your children are going to have a fellowship with kids in the neighborhood automatically because they're going to play with each other, we can't stop them from doing that, and we don't want to stop them."

Today, many public schools are shockingly segregated and the inequalities between majority-white schools and majority-non-white schools are equally shocking. Recently one report found that "nationally, predominantly white school districts get $23 billion more than their nonwhite peers, despite serving a similar number of children."[5]

The integration of schools has crawled along ever since *Brown v. Board of Education*. But at this moment in time, there's an opportunity to further integrate schools. Recent patterns in migration in the US see many white people moving into urban areas, and many people of color moving to the suburbs, and as a result, racial diversity in public schools is happening more frequently.

The positive outcomes of racially diverse schools that John talks about aren't wishful thinking or idealized projections. Findings have shown the positive impacts on school performance for all kids, white and non-white, who are a part of diverse schools.[6] Children of color don't need white kids *more* than white kids need children of color. The benefits are mutual.

Of course for any change to take place it will require people with privilege, namely middle-class white Christians, to choose to integrate their children in schools with children of color. And to do that we would have to believe that we're connected each other, all possessing the image of God.

John said it this way, "We're sort of in this world as Christians together and that God calls us to love our neighbors as we love ourselves. And God calls us to be redemptive. What a privilege it is for you and me to be working together with God among the underprivileged, because he says that 'If you help the poor, you are lending to the Lord,'[7] which means that there is a return in eternity and that is a biblical idea that's not lost on Scripture. We want a good quality of life, and Jesus said I've come that you may have life and may have it more abundantly, so God wants us to have a qualitative meaningful life but he doesn't want it by the exploitation of other people."

---

5. EdBuild, "$23 Billion," 4.
6. Wells et al., "How Racially Diverse Schools."
7. Proverbs 19:17, NLT.

"Sounds like there is a responsibility when someone moves into a neighborhood predominantly of a different culture," I reasoned.

John said, "The blessing that God shares with you there is a *tremendous* responsibility! I'll be eighty-four soon, but man, I'm not getting any poorer, and my friends who I know whose heart is with God are not getting any poorer. There's this idea of serving God so he can make you rich. That's not quite what's happening. David can say things like, 'I was young and now I am old, yet I have never seen the righteous forsaken or their children begging bread.'[8] I'm not serving God to obtain wealth. I'm serving God in gratitude as I see him keep his promises."

Health and Nutrition

"Dr. Perkins, I know that physical health is another area where people of color have faced racism, but it's been hard for some to understand how that could be. I remember how your wife, Vera Mae, pointed out in *A Quiet Revolution*[9] that African Americans only had a two-burner oil stove and so nothing they ate could be baked, only fried because it was the only way they had to cook it. It may be a smaller thing when compared to the fullness of the hardships that people of color in America have had to endure, but health is such a basic factor for humans."

Statistically Black Americans have higher rates of heart disease. It seems systemic racism forced many Black Americans into poverty, which limited them to only a two-burner oil stove and frying, which in turn led to health issues.

John picked up the conversational thread. "Yeah, consider the time it takes to bake compared to frying, and add to that the cost of the gas to bake with compared to frying on a wood-burning stove. Frying food was just the way of life, and now we've developed a taste for that. Being too poor to do anything but fry is what really

8. Psalm 37:25, NIV.
9. Perkins, *A Quiet Revolution*.

brought on problems with diabetes. Many times women would get pregnant and never get tested for diabetes."

Considering the care that we know should be taken during pregnancy, I realized that this was no small inequity, especially considering birth defects, preeclampsia, still births, maternal death rates, and other risks involved with diabetes in pregnancy.

"Vera Mae's family had diabetes," John told me. "They couldn't afford anything else, so they were left to frying as the only method of cooking. Also, the taste, they got used to that taste, that's why the fast-food thing works because there's a taste that goes with that grease."

"What about healthcare?" I asked. "I've heard of statistics about African Americans having less access to healthcare and going to the doctor less, especially African American men. Is there a connection between those statistics and the way doctor's offices ran in the 1960s and earlier? I know they had separate waiting rooms, and Black people would be seen after the last white person was seen, and they could be left waiting all day."

"Yes, that is part of it. These systemic issues really hurt Black people. I want to be redemptive and forgiving, but at the same time recognize that discrimination and systemic injustice happened."

John was articulating something important. We can name injustices *and* show love and forgiveness. They are not opposites. In fact, naming the injustice might be a necessary part of forgiveness.

Michael Brown

On this particular day that John and I were talking, the nation was reeling from the shooting of Michael Brown, an unarmed eighteen-year-old, by police officer Darren Wilson in Ferguson, Missouri. In the aftermath protesters took to the streets in Ferguson. Many of the protests were peaceful, while some weren't. The unrest reverberated throughout the country. *Christianity Today* had just published a short interview they did with John about the situation.

"I read your interview in *Christianity Today*, about what's happened in Ferguson, Missouri in the aftermath of the murder of Michael Brown."[10]

"Oh yeah, I did a little interview. I think I saw it in print."

"You did a great job with it. I like how you mentioned that a good multicultural church in that town could have brought some peace in the aftermath."

"Yes, multiracial churches and people of color in positions of power. That's what they did in the end. They had to reach out to find a Black highway patrolman who had been born in Ferguson, and to bring him back there to make him the spokesman."

"I saw that."

"They didn't have but three Black policemen on the force," he said incredulously.

"Which is crazy for a police force of that size in a community with that high of a percentage of people of color," I replied.

"I didn't know the state of that department, but then you read about one of the white policemen on the force saying, 'I'm . . . a killer'[11] and city officials talked all of that racial stuff about Obama.[12] I saw on the news one of the Black girls who was protesting was saying, 'We're not going to continue on with this few Blacks on the force.' Going forward what they have to do is train both the Black and the white officers on how to be men and women of respect and dignity."

The police officer John cited was Dan Page. He was suspended from the Ferguson police department after a video surfaced of a bizarre speech Page gave at a meeting of Oath Keepers, a group that describes itself as "a non-partisan association of current and formerly serving military, police, and first responders, who pledge to fulfill the oath all military and police take to 'defend the Constitution against all enemies, foreign and domestic.'"[13] Many

---

10. Becker, "John Perkins."

11. Lookup Wakeup, "Red Alert!!!"

12. U.S. Department of Justice, "Investigation of the Ferguson Police Department," 72.

13. Oath Keepers, "About Oath Keepers."

outside the organization see Oath Keepers as a heavily armed, far-right group prone to militia activity.

Page's rambling speech contained conspiracy theories and derogatory language about Muslims. The speech also contained the quote that John referenced:

> I personally believe in Jesus Christ as my lord and savior, but I'm also a killer . . . I've killed a lot. And if I need to, I'll kill a whole bunch more. If you don't want to get killed, don't show up in front of me. I have no problems with it. God did not raise me to be a coward . . . I'm into diversity—I kill everybody. I don't care.[14]

The scariest part about Page's speech is that this man ostensibly held these ideologies while patrolling the streets of St. Louis County as an officer for more than twenty years.

John knows the real stakes that arise when law enforcement agencies lack diversity. He's told me that he generally doesn't fear members of law enforcement like he used to after being beaten by the highway patrol in Brandon, and that's partly because of the changes many agencies have made. In John's mind, if he were taken to jail today he would expect there would be at least one Black patrolman around. "It wouldn't be all white patrolmen there, and so they couldn't torture me to the same extent they did back in 1970."

Blind Loyalty to Law Enforcement

It was early fall, and it was still warm outside. I was at John's house in Jackson. I liked to get as much in-person time with him as I could. We were sitting at his dining room table having just finished lunch, and talking about what was going on in the world.

"I don't know if you saw, but somebody made a GoFundMe account to raise money for Darren Wilson, and it raised its goal in a couple of days, from people ready to show their support."[15]

14. Lookup Wakeup, "Red Alert!!!"
15. Over 1 million dollars was raised for Darren Wilson in the end.

Darren Wilson was the police officer that killed Michael Brown. I felt strange telling John, like I was breaking bad news. But of course he had seen it all. He knew how low people could stoop.

"Yes, I could imagine that. It's a part of the fall, too. In addition to the cultural behavior, it's a part of the fall, to follow our selfish desire, to follow what we desire to be. See, that creates more sin. If somebody is enough of a racist, they would desire that white folks dominate our authority structures, since that has been the custom of our time. You follow me?"

"Yes," I nodded.

"They want that custom to be okay. Of course, white folks feel safe when a white policeman pulls them over. They don't feel, automatically, like they're going to be beaten. A Black person *will* feel that. I know I have felt that."

"As I said, it was only with time, after I got out of the Brandon jail . . ." John trailed off. Then he regathered his thoughts. "Even though I made the commitment to love whites, Blacks, and to preach the gospel, when I got out of jail, I didn't want to do that. It took some time for me to work out and live up to my commitment that I had made. I still could feel that fear, even though I had made a commitment that I didn't want to fear, I did."

Mike Brown is just one of several unarmed Black people killed by police in the last several years. Each one exposes a deep racial division in the US. A cycle begins: most white people take the side of police and most Black people take the side of the victim. Each time we hear the same things: "don't break the law and you won't have anything to worry about," "just comply." But, most Black people know, it may not matter if you break the law or not, and complying with police is not a guarantee that things will be justly sorted out later, or that law enforcement won't act out violently anyway. These are the lived experiences of people of color and very few white people have experienced the same thing themselves, so many white people conclude that people of color must be exaggerating or overreacting. We fail to trust and believe the experiences of people of color and live in what author Drew Hart calls "counterintuitive solidarity."[16]

> White American Christians in our society must do something seemingly absurd and unnatural, yet very Christian in orientation: they must move decisively toward a counterintuitive solidarity with those on the margins. They must allow the eyes of the violated of the land to lead and guide them, seeking to have renewed minds no longer conformed to the patterns of our world.[17]

Counterintuitive solidarity is a tool that allows those of us who don't have "eyes to see" the ability to borrow the eyes of others through trusting their stories.

Choosing not to live in counterintuitive solidarity is not simply morally neutral. It keeps the harmful systems in place, it dehumanizes, it pours salt in the open wound of those hurting from the violence of these incidents, and is itself a new wound.

I've known many good people in law enforcement. They are selfless and want to honestly protect and serve. The point of talking about the recent and distant history of the relationship between people of color and law enforcement is not to set police up as enemies or to persuade anyone to be "anti-cop," but to simply acknowledge the narrative that most white people have about law enforcement officials is an incomplete story.

John Shares: What We Do in the Face of History

"Dr. Perkins, all these things we've been talking about: racism in healthcare, education, and criminal justice, I don't know if anything is going to change until white Christians acknowledge their part in it now and throughout history." I stared out the window, just letting my admission hang in the air.

I think John could sense my discouragement. As usual, when he spoke his voice was steady and exuded compassion. "Well,

16. Hart, *Trouble I've Seen*.
17. Hart, *Trouble I've Seen*, 87.

Shane, I think those barriers to understanding are breaking down. How wonderful is it for us to have the task of encouraging people to use that privilege *for* others, invest *in* others with that privilege, and to trust God for the extension of that privilege to everyone. I hope that God would find white Christians as faithful servants, and he promised that if we invest what we have he will give back to the giver, although not in worldly ways."

"In Luke 17, Jesus tells a parable about the bad steward who says to himself, 'I will tear down these barns and I will build bigger ones to store my surplus grains.'[18] The idea of the harvest was very good but he was using that harvest only for himself."

"The church should be rescuing the perishing, caring for the dying, and being redemptive within our society, that's what we want and that's what we've got to encourage. So the churches that I interact with are doing some new things and trying to be some of that change we want to see. We're not just accusing others. That's what you and I could be doing right now, we could be just accusing others and feeling a little bit better about ourselves. That's not what we want. We want to live a life of sharing some of that brokenness within society."

"I think you and I sitting here right now are exposing the fallacy of neutral living. We want the oppressed to join together with us to make life better. You know a lot of the people who ask me to come and speak and work with their organization, they reach out to me because they think I live a pretty good life, but they are so addicted to themselves. They want me to help them, but they don't want us to act together. They will say things like 'I can serve God just as well at home' but they come to me, someone who has been nurtured by the church, and I just want to say to them, 'Well, sister/brother I want you to join with us, and what a joy it would be to be working together with God to carry on this redemptive work on earth.'"

John's words were typical of the way he talks—challenging yet gracious, self-giving yet with clear boundaries. All of this makes me wonder what I'm doing with my privilege. Most middle-class

18. Luke 17:18, paraphrase.

Americans are in the top 10 percent of the world's wealthiest people, but even most millionaires don't see themselves as rich.[19] I confess that my household income is an amount that several years ago I thought would make me "comfortable," but now that it's been attained I still feel like we're just scraping by. Is that because of the rising cost of housing (especially in my neck of the woods), and healthcare, among other necessities, or is it that it is the American way of life is to have a lot and feel like you have a little? Do things really cost that much more, or do we simply buy more things when our income increases, and then suddenly believe that those things we started buying, that we used to do without, are now necessities?

Much ink has been spilled about privilege as it pertains to race, and rightfully so. The privilege that is afforded to white people, and denied to people of color in much of the world, is glaring. The question is, what to do with it. I would think that for followers of Jesus, we should be willing to take his lead and lay it down. In fact, we're commanded to in Philippians 2:4–8:

> Let each of you look not to your own interests, but to
> the interests of others. Let the same mind be in you that
> was in Christ Jesus,
> who, though he was in the form of God,
>   did not regard equality with God
>   as something to be exploited,
> but emptied himself,
>   taking the form of a slave,
>   being born in human likeness.
> And being found in human form,
>   he humbled himself
>   and became obedient to the point of death–
>   even death on a cross.

Jesus Christ, it turns out, is the picture of privilege laid down, and he invites us to do likewise.

---

19. Ameriprise Financial Services, LLC, "Building wealth."

Going Deeper

1. Were you taught things in school about history, that weren't true, or omitted certain facts about past injustices toward people of color?

2. Why is it important for people to know the history of race in America and the rest of the world?

3. What advantages or disadvantages have you had as a result of systemic injustice?

4. What systemic injustices toward people of color do you see happening today?

Further Reading

- *Prophetic Lament: A Call for Justice in Troubled Times*, by Soong-Chan Rah

- *White Awake: An Honest Look at What It Means to Be White*, by Daniel Hill

- *The New Jim Crow: Mass Incarceration in the Age of Color-blindness*, by Michelle Alexander

- *Rethinking Incarceration: Advocating for Justice That Restores*, by Dominique DuBois Gilliard

- *The Myth of Equality: Uncovering the Roots of Injustice and Privilege*, by Ken Wytsma

CHAPTER 9

We Must Be the Church

John's Belief in the Incarnate Body of Christ

I F YOU'VE BEEN A part of the church long enough you've been hurt by the church. Gossip, betrayal, sexual impropriety, judgmentalism, racism, homogeneity, and greed have destroyed churches and the people that are a part of them. It's enough to understand why many throw their hands in the air, and walk away from the church, or allow the church to walk away from them.

I used to think that the American expression of the church was especially and uniquely flawed, as if it had committed transgressions that had never been committed before. But then I remember that some of the earliest letters to churches, Paul's epistles, were written to correct churches of their misdeeds and shortcomings, some of them the very same issues we struggle with today. What I suspect is that the modern day churches' shortcomings are not so much a recent sickness, but something that will be a part of a gathering of imperfect people. This in no way excuses the misdeeds of some people in the church, some of them horrific. Dietrich Bonhoeffer elaborates on it this way: "Those who love their dream of a Christian community more than they love the Christian community itself become destroyers of that Christian community even though their personal intentions may be ever so honest, earnest and sacrificial."[1] What Bonhoeffer is saying to me is that my short patience with the church may come from good intentions, but it is actually destroying it.

So how do we move forward while loving the church, and calling it to faithfulness? I knew that John's lifetime of devotion to the church, in the face of repeated disappointment and betrayal, could help me forge some sort of path.

John Shares: The Church

I was again in my house in Austin, sitting at my desk in the "nurffice," talking to John. Truthfully, the lackluster view out the window of my neighbor's fence about three feet away and some stray tree limbs was perfect because it gave me something to look at while not stealing my focus. "Dr. Perkins, you've traveled to churches around the world and throughout the country, how has that left you feeling about the church?"

"Well, on that recent trip I took to Malaysia I learned so much. I learned that we're becoming one world! You know, a bunch of our behavior in the world is taking on a sense of sameness, most of the world is wearing the same kind of T-shirts and pants we're wearing, and hip-hop culture is all over the world now. I see famous musicians here are the same musicians there. Music is making it one world."

"The other thing I learned is that Malaysians are breaking through the traditional barriers, including ethnic barriers, and they're doing it without visible structures. Big cities are building high rises and churches are going in, renting out either an apartment or a recreation center, and the church can thrive there. They're not building church buildings that much like we are here, so most of their resources can go to fund amazing stuff in the world."

"Wow!" I replied. "Are they able to worship freely in Malaysia or is there pushback from the government?"

---

1. Bonhoeffer, *Life Together*, 36.

"Islam is recognized as the official religion. It's against the law for Christians or anybody else to evangelize openly or to get a Muslim to convert. I don't know all the details of that, but I believe what happens under these circumstances is that people are more serious about making a decision to follow Christ because they realize the consequences of what that choice could mean for them. The possibility of persecution has *always* been a part of the church throughout history. Our current time in the United States is unusual in that regard. At times, Christ has revealed himself, people have responded, and throughout history, some have burned at the stake for it."

What John's describing isn't unique. Historically the Christian church has grown when it was on the margins of society. It seems that when Christians are offered the possibility of worldly power and privilege that Christianity becomes domesticated and compromised. It's important not to romanticize persecution, but it's equally important not waste time on persecution paranoia as much of the church in the United States has.

What Is the Church Really?

You can't be around John for too long before you hear him talk about the church. To him, the church is not a nice add-on for Christians involved in social justice. He sees the work of the church involving both our collective inward spiritual selves and our embodiment of Jesus in the world through social justice, and for him, those can't be separated. He believes the *reason* to accept Jesus as your Lord and Savior, or whatever terminology you want to use to describe being a Jesus-follower, is of course to obtain peace between ourselves and God, but also so that we can get busy partnering with God in the work of rescue, renewal, and reconciliation in the world.

Ugandan Catholic priest and theologian Emmanuel Katongole and coauthor Chris Rice write in *Reconciling All Things* about the unique work the church can do and has done in the world in remedying injustice. They refer to the "gap" between what is and what should be:

> Another gift God gives is the church and Christian community. Of course the church is always full of problems and weakness. Yet it is critical for leaders to obediently connect themselves in faith to her vitality and gifts. By being grounded in the church's life and worship and in the unique story and vision she alone holds, we are shaped within journey, task, and community that is bigger than "me" and "my'" gap. There is no public Mother Teresa without the one who, until recently, remained hidden. Her private journals reveal a world of spiritual retreats and directors, prayers full of tears and wrestling with God, bishops putting her vision to the test, disciplines of transparency and reflection, and a community that corrected, nourished and encouraged her. In learning to belong to a community, we learn to return our work to God.[2]

John explained to me specifically what he saw as the mandate of the church. "You have to understand the work of the church is to equip the saints for the work of the ministry, that's pretty plain when you think about it. The work of ministry is to rescue the perishing, care for the dying, *that's* amazing grace at work in the lives of people. The church equips us for that. Jesus didn't write a book. He lived a life and his followers communicated to us what he was saying, and why he was saying it. Isn't that powerful? It's a powerful institution but our differences have us divided, whether we're man or woman, what race we are, or our economic status."

I then had to interject with a bit of vulnerability. "I know I told you before, but my family and I have been looking for new churches here in town. Because of my relationship with you and other people of color, as well as some things that I've read and learned, I've come to believe that multicultural church isn't just nice but necessary."

John said, "I think one of the words of wisdom I would give you is: when you visit a new church, ask yourself—'Is there

2. Katongole and Rice, *Reconciling All Things*, 139.

a mission here that I could buy into?' It's easy to join a church because we prefer the preaching or the music, but when the quality of the preaching or music disappears, we're too willing to just leave and find another church that fits my new preference, my desire. And often worship style is a big superficial difference between a white church and a Black church, but worship styles shouldn't have the final say. So look for a church with a deeper mission, not just to a single issue, but to a holistic commitment to the gospel. We put things where our heart is. Do you see what I'm talking about, Shane?"

"I do. That's beautiful." I realized, if my heart is for the gospel (and I hope it is), then it makes no sense to chase a style of worship, or a "dynamic kids' ministry." My commitment needed to be deeper than that.

"You know, Dr. Perkins, for most of us in America"—I was thinking out loud as I often did with John—"there are so many choices of churches we could go to, whereas, you think about the early church, they were such a minority that they couldn't squabble over little things. They certainly couldn't split up over their race or ethnicity."

"Right. Of course. Christians today have to bring the church back to a better identity. Who are we? I think that question was being asked in the New Testament. Peter was saying that to the Christians when he said 'ye are a chosen generation, a royal priesthood, holy nation, a peculiar people; that ye should shew forth the praises of him who hath called you out of darkness into his marvelous light.'"[3]

"The problem is that we're not 'peculiar people,' instead, we make Christianity out to be a civil religion. We expect society to behave as we behave. I don't think that we can 'behave' without God being with us and without the church."

John was right. He was helping me yet again to make sense of the questions I had and the problems I was facing. We *do* make Christianity a civil religion. Sometimes I wonder if Christians would really hate a country that truly behaves "like Christ." Would

3. 1 Peter 2:9, KJV.

we really like a country full of people who reject violence, eschew wealth, and love their enemies? We tell ourselves that our worldview is based on our Christian values. Is it that or is it that we want to hang on to a world that looks like the one we grew up in, or maybe create a new one made in our own image. The writer David Foster Wallace told a parable in his address to the graduating class at Kenyon College in 2005:

> There are these two young fish swimming along, and they happen to meet an older fish swimming the other way, who nods at them and says, "Morning, boys. How's the water?" And the two young fish swim on for a bit, and then eventually one of them looks over at the other and goes, "What the hell is water?"[4]

I think this is why Paul says in Romans 2:12 not to "be conformed to this world, but be transformed by the renewing of your minds, so that you may discern what is the will of God—what is good and acceptable and perfect." He knew that one's culture is the water they swim in and we don't even see how we're shaped or "conformed" by it. And the only way we can keep from being conformed by it is by the constant renewing of our minds. I'm not just talking about the larger national culture, but also our microculture, whatever that is for you: that progressive, city-dwelling, bike-riding, coffee-drinking culture, or that conservative, pickup-driving, cargo short-wearing, Cracker Barrel-eating culture. Microcultures are the most blinding. To me I know my mind is being renewed and not conformed when I start believing in things I'm uncomfortable with. That's the only way that I know of to realize that a belief is coming from outside of myself. Everyone should believe in some theology that they aren't 100 percent comfortable with. If your theology always matches your personality, and especially your microculture, you should be worried. The church should be a place where our minds can be transformed. A place where we're confronted with reality.

4. Wallace, "This is Water."

The Pain Churches Have Caused

I know that many people have been wounded by the church. In fact some of the most heinous acts in the news in the last several years have been perpetrated by those *leading* churches and covered up *by* the church. I have no interest in glossing over those injustices. When those in the church behave badly, we need to be the first to name it and hold the perpetrators accountable. A church shouldn't be a place where bad actors find a harbor from their consequences. The church should care for the victims first and foremost and ensure that they feel safe.

It's important to remember that when we rightfully give blame to the church for its failures, we should give credit when it's due as well. I know there have been many churches where leaders have been able to commit terrible acts of sexual assault and manipulation against adults and children. I also know of Christians who work for justice for those victims. Many churches have made certain groups outcasts and marginalized them. I know people who are working to care for those that society has decided they have no use for, and they are caring for them because the story of Jesus has compelled them to.

I've encountered so many people that have been so beaten up by the church, and they are so embarrassed by what they see happening in the world in the name of Christianity that, although they still have a connection to Jesus, they would no longer use the word *Christian* to describe themselves. Author and pastor Jonathan Martin says, "If we hand our sons & daughters a faith exposed as misogynistic, racist, unconcerned about creation & the poor—they aren't wrong to leave it."[5] But we need to understand that it's not real Christianity that they/we are leaving. It was a poor impostor. An important lesson to take away is that we can't let cynicism rule our lives and ruin beautiful things.

Some churches are far from the heart of God. I've seen them. But I've also seen something else. For every bullying, money-hungry, egotistical, high-profile pastor, there are 100 you'll never

5. Martin, Twitter post.

hear of because they are busy putting their heads down and loving the people around them. For every church concerned with status, many others are simply trying to figure out how to best follow Jesus and care for their community.

All churches are flawed. They all fail in some area. They will all let someone down at some point. They are made up of imperfect people. Another quote from Dietrich Bonhoeffer reminds us:

> The community of the saints is not an "ideal" community consisting of perfect and sinless men and women, where there is no need for further repentance. No, it is a community that proves that it is worthy of the gospel of forgiveness by constantly and sincerely proclaiming God's forgiveness . . . Sanctification means driving out the world from the Church as well as separating the Church from the world. But the purpose of such discipline is not to establish a community of the perfect, but a community consisting of men who live under the forgiving mercy of God.[6]

What Church Can Be

In the book of Acts, we're given a snapshot in time of a church as a beautiful extension of Jesus.

> They devoted themselves to the apostles' teaching and fellowship, to the breaking of bread and the prayers. Awe came upon everyone, because many wonders and signs were being done by the apostles. All who believed were together and had all things in common; they would sell their possessions and goods and distribute the proceeds to all, as any had need. Day by day, as they spent much time together in the temple, they broke bread at home and ate their food with glad and generous hearts, praising God and having the goodwill of all the people. And day by day

6. Bonhoeffer, *The Cost of Discipleship*, 287.

the Lord added to their number those who were being saved.[7]

No church is perfect, including this early church in the book of Acts. Still, there are lessons we can learn both from this church and those today that are doing what they can to be a faithful picture of God's people.

John told me about a church in Jackson called One Church.[8] One Church was launched with diversity as a deeply held value. The church is involved in several incarnational activities, including delivering school supplies and healthy foods to children and families living nearby, while also leading them in Bible studies and prayer. One Church also advocates for immigrants living nearby.

Churches that want to change and eschew homogeneity don't have to reinvent the wheel. Some churches have gone before them and there are resources. Mosaix is one organization that exists as a resource for pastors and organizations that want to be diverse. "Mosaix is a relational network of pastors and planters, denominational and network leaders, educators, authors, and researchers alike, that exists to establish healthy multiethnic and economically diverse, culturally intelligent, socially just, and financially sustainable churches that express a credible witness of God's love for all people in an increasingly diverse, painfully polarized, and cynical society."[9]

Priorities Matter

I see many Christians gravitate toward large churches, especially ones with large and elaborate children's ministries because their children like being there. I admire people who go to a church they don't connect with because they have a "good kids ministry," but what I think kids need most in a church are parents who come alive inside of it. Many times the churches that are being

7. Acts 2:42–47, NRSV.
8. One Church, "Welcome to One Church For All People."
9. Mosaix, "About Mosaix Global Network."

incarnational aren't the biggest in town, and sometimes aren't large at all. There's nothing wrong with large churches per se, but we have to ask ourselves if what we're attracted to in those churches is the "bigness" itself. It might be time to rearrange our priorities and put incarnational activities at the top of that list. There is most likely a church in your town that is busy joining God in his work in the world, preaching a holistic gospel.

Going Deeper

1. What are some ways that you've seen the church fail to bring about racial justice?

2. What does it mean to you to hear about churches like One Church and organizations like Mosaix?

3. Think about your own church. Does the leadership reflect the diversity of your community, or the kingdom of God itself?

Further Reading

*   *Reconciling All Things: A Christian Vision for Justice, Peace and Healing,* by Emmanuel Katongole and Chris Rice

*   *Trouble I've Seen: Changing the Way the Church Views Racism,* by Drew G. I. Hart

*   *Mirror to the Church: Resurrecting Faith after Genocide in Rwanda,* by Emmanuel M. Katongole

Bibliography

Ameriprise Financial Services, LLC. "Building wealth is a journey even for millionaires." *Modern Money,* part II, infographic, December 11–25, 2018. https://www.ameriprise.com/financial-news-research/studies/modern-money-infographic.

Barber, Leroy. *Red, Brown, Yellow, Black, White—Who's More Precious In God's Sight? A Call for Diversity in Christian Missions and Ministry.* New York: Jericho, 2014.

Becker, Amy Julia. "John Perkins: The Sin of Racism Made Ferguson Escalate So Quickly." *Christianity Today,* August 2014. https://www.christianitytoday.com/amyjuliabecker/2014/august/john-perkins-sin-of-racism-made-ferguson-escalate-so-quickl.html.

Bonhoeffer, Dietrich. *The Cost of Discipleship.* New York: Touchstone, 1995.

———. *Life Together: The Classic Exploration of Christian in Community.* San Francisco: HarperOne, 2009.

Brown, Brené. *Braving the Wilderness: The Quest for True Belonging and the Courage to Stand Alone.* New York: Random, 2017.

Dougherty, Kevin D., and Michael O. Emerson. "The Changing Complexion of American Congregations." *Journal for the Scientific Study of Religion.* https://doi.org/10.1111/jssr.12495.

EdBuild. "$23 Billion." https://edbuild.org/content/23-billion.

Farley, Robert. "Is Illegal Immigration Linked to More or Less Crime?" FactCheck.org, June 27, 2018. https://www.factcheck.org/2018/06/is-illegal-immigration-linked-to-more-or-less-crime/.

Hart, Drew. *Trouble I've Seen: Changing the Way the Church Views Racism.* Harrisonburg, PA: Herald, 2016.

Katongole, Emmanuel, and Chris Rice. *Reconciling All Things: A Christian Vision for Justice, Peace and Healing.* Downers Grove, IL: InterVarsity, 2008.

King, Martin Luther, Jr. "'I Have A Dream' Speech, In Its Entirety." March on Washington for Jobs and Freedom, Washington, DC, August 28, 1963.

https://www.npr.org/2010/01/18/122701268/i-have-a-dream-speech-in-its-entirety.

Lookup Wakeup. "Red Alert!!! Sgt Major Dan Page the truth of America." https://www.youtube.com/watch?v=0jFtXG4fC5A.

Martin, Jonathan (@theboyonthebike). "If we hand our sons & daughters a faith exposed as misogynistic, racist, unconcerned about creation & the poor-they aren't wrong to leave it." Twitter, April 19, 2017. https://twitter.com/theboyonthebike/status/854844759344644096?lang=en.

Mobile Loaves & Fishes. "About Us." https://mlf.org/us/.

Mosaix. "About Mosaix Global Network." https://mosaix.info/about-mosaix/.

Moynihan, Daniel. "The Negro Family: The Case for National Action." US Department of Labor, 1965. https://www.dol.gov/general/aboutdol/history/webid-moynihan.

Nowrasteh, Alex. "Illegal Immigrants and Crime—Assessing the Evidence." Cato Institute, March 4, 2019. https://www.cato.org/blog/illegal-immigrants-crime-assessing-evidence.

Oath Keepers. "About Oath Keepers." https://oathkeepers.org/about/.

One Church. "Welcome to One Church For All People." https://thatonechurch.org/.

Perkins, John M. Let Justice Roll Down. Grand Rapids: Baker, 2012.

———. A Quiet Revolution. Pasadena, CA: Urban Family, 1976.

———. With Justice for All: A Strategy for Community Development. Grand Rapids: Baker, 2014.

Perkins, Spencer, and Chris Rice. More Than Equals: Racial Healing for the Sake of the Gospel. Rev. ed. Downers Grove, IL: InterVarsity, 2000.

Pyke, Karen D. "What Is Internalized Racial Oppression and Why Don't We Study It? Acknowledging Racism's Hidden Injuries." Sociological Perspectives 53, no. 4 (December 2010) 551–72. https://doi.org/10.1525/sop.2010.53.4.551.

Rah, Soong-Chan. Prophetic Lament: A Call for Justice in Troubled Times. Downers Grove, IL: InterVarsity, 2015.

Reilly, Katie. "Here Are All the Times Donald Trump Insulted Mexico." Time, January 25, 2021. https://time.com/4473972/donald-trump-mexico-meeting-insult/.

Stevenson, Bryan. "We need to talk about an injustice." TED Talk, 23:17. March 1, 2012. https://www.ted.com/talks/bryan_stevenson_we_need_to_talk_about_an_injustice#t-5245.

Toussaint, Loren L., Everett Worthington, Jr., and David R. Williams, eds. Forgiveness and Health: Scientific Evidence and Theories Relating Forgiveness to Better Health. Dordrecht: Springer, 2015.

U.S. Department of Justice, Civil Rights Division. "Investigation of the Ferguson Police Department." https://www.justice.gov/sites/default/files/opa/press-releases/attachments/2015/03/04/ferguson_police_department_report.pdf.

Wallace, David Foster. "This is Water." Commencement Speech, Kenyon College, Gambier, Ohio, May 21, 2005. https://web/ics.purdue.edu/~drkelly/DFWKenyonAddress2005.pdf.

Weir, Kirsten. "Forgiveness can improve mental and physical health: Research shows how to get there." *American Psychological Association* 48 (January 2017) 64–69. https://www.apa.org/monitor/2017/01/ce-corner.

Wells, Amy Stuart, Lauren Fox, and Diana Cordova-Cobo. "How Racially Diverse Schools and Classrooms Can Benefit All Students." https://tcf.org/content/report/how-racially-diverse-schools-and-classrooms-can-benefit-all-students/.

White, Dan, Jr. *Love Over Fear: Facing Monsters, Befriending Enemies, and Healing Our Polarized World.* Chicago: Moody, 2019.